Cooking for children

For Corentin, Timothée, Tanguy and Victoire, with all my love.

Trish Deseine

cooking for
children

Photographs: Sylvain Thomas

Stylist: Trish Deseine

HACHETTE
Illustrated

This is not just a cookbook for children...

… but one for the people who feed them. For mothers, obviously, but also for the other people who inhabit their lives: fathers, nannies, grandparents and parents of friends, people who do the shopping, organize their time and find themselves responsible for what goes into their tummies.

This book does not transform feeding four- to twelve-year olds into a creative hobby. Cooking is such an important part of our lives that learning how to cook cannot be confined to baking sessions on a Wednesday afternoon. In this book you won't find a mouse with a rice pudding body, currants for eyes and an orange rind tail, or a pizza decorated to resemble a teddy bear.

What you will find, however, is a host of very simple recipes that older children will be able to make on their own, together with suggestions for times when everyone can help with the cooking in a natural and spontaneous way. But more importantly, this book contains ideas arranged around OUR moods and OUR constraints as adults.

We cook as we live. During the week, we don't have much time and preparing the evening meal is often viewed as a chore. At the weekend and on holiday, on the other hand, time is no longer at a premium: cooking suddenly becomes an almost cultural activity. We experience an intense pleasure in going to the market, discovering new ingredients, inventing dishes and rediscovering a serene, sharing atmosphere.

And then, from time to time, there is reason to celebrate. We enjoy ourselves and bring pleasure to the people around us. Birthday teas, celebrations with friends, cakes to make for school: cooking becomes fun, dramatic, excessive, and often very sweet! This way of cooking, even if it is reserved for special occasions, is just as necessary as all the rest, because it prevents the frustration that can subsequently go on to develop into bad habits.

Cooking for Children is a collection of realistic, easy, varied, creative and, I hope, fun recipes and ideas. Because, although food is a serious matter, nothing should stop us from taking pleasure in cooking it!

Plenty of time

... for cooking, of course, and specifically to cook the recipes in this chapter without the pressure of time!

Some of the special recipes may require a little more time because their unusual ingredients may take time to track down. To help on this score I have included a list of retail outlets on page 192.

The most essential requirement of these dishes is that the children spend time trying, tasting and discovering new combinations of flavours and taste sensations. It is also up to us to make the time to explain the recipe to them, to let them help us make it and then to spend a happy mealtime together at the table.

Hot or cold cream of lettuce soup with peas

Serves 4
Preparation time: 10 minutes
Cooking time: 1½ hours, including stock

For the stock:
30 g (1 oz) unsalted butter
500 g (1 lb) carrots, peeled and sliced
4 celery sticks, with leaves, chopped
500 g (1 lb) onions, chopped
2 litres (3½ pints) cold water
1 bouquet garni

For the soup:
200 g (7 oz) Little Gem, Cos,
or any other lettuce hearts, chopped
150 ml (¼ pint) single cream
salt and freshly ground black pepper
150 g (5 oz) peas, steamed or boiled until just cooked

For the stock: melt the butter in a large pan, add the vegetables and cook gently, without allowing them to colour. Add the water and the bouquet garni, then bring to the boil. Simmer over a low heat for at least 1 hour. Pass the stock through a sieve – you should have about 1 litre (1¾ pints) of stock.

For the soup: bring the stock to the boil, add the lettuce and simmer for 10 to 15 minutes. When the lettuce is soft, blend it and the stock in a liquidizer. Stir in the cream, salt and pepper and finally the peas and serve hot or cold.

Fig and smoked salmon salad

Just one way of serving figs when they are in season, as an interesting alternative to the more traditional cured ham.

Serves 4
Preparation time: 2 minutes

4 large, ripe figs
4 slices organic smoked salmon

Cut the figs into quarters and serve with the slices of smoked salmon and a few slices of toasted multi-grain bread.

Salad of griddled and dried pears with smoked tuna

Serves 4
Preparation time: 5 minutes

1 large pear, sliced lengthways
4 dried pears, cut into pieces
100 g (3½ oz) smoked tuna

Sear the pear slices on a griddle.

Serve warm with the dried pears and slices of smoked tuna.

If using canned tuna, drain well first.

Coco's carpaccio with oven chips

This is a dish my oldest son loves making both for himself and for all the family. The recipe is a good way of showing that preparing meat in a different way can totally change how people enjoy it.

Chips cooked in the oven are less fatty than those cooked in a deep-fat fryer. You can also chop up some carrots, sweet potatoes and celeriac and cook them with the potatoes.

Serves 4
Preparation time: 20 minutes
Cooking time: 25 minutes

good quality olive oil
500 g (1 lb) potatoes, peeled and cut into large chips
300 g (12 oz) carpaccio of beef and/or veal
lemon juice
Parmesan cheese shavings
fresh basil
sea salt
freshly ground black pepper

Preheat the oven to 190°C (375°F), gas mark 5.

Drizzle the olive oil over the potatoes and roast for 20 to 25 minutes, turning regularly.

Arrange the meat on the plates, drizzle with the lemon juice and garnish with Parmesan shavings, basil, salt and pepper.

Prawn cakes

Serves 4
Preparation time: 10 minutes
Cooking time: 5 minutes

1 spring onion
1 small garlic clove
rind and juice of 2 limes
pinch of sugar
1 tablespoon fresh coriander
375 g (12 oz) peeled, uncooked prawns
2 tablespoons plain flour
2 tablespoons sunflower oil

Place all the ingredients, except for the oil, in a mini-food chopper or food processor and purée briefly so that the mixture retains some texture.

On a lightly floured surface, shape the mixture into small cakes. Heat the oil in a frying pan and fry the cakes for a few minutes on each side until golden.

Serve with sweet-and-sour or sweet chilli sauces as dips, Mangetout peas with peanuts (see page 176), and rice or Thai noodles.

Potatoes with sweet chilli sauce

Serves 4
Preparation time: 10 minutes
Cooking time: 40 minutes

500 g (1 lb) potatoes
4 tablespoons olive oil
1 tablespoon spice mixture (such as Moroccan
ras el hanout, Thai 7-spice mixture, ground cumin,
curry powder)
sea salt
2–3 tablespoons sweet chilli sauce (available from the
oriental food section of your supermarket)

Preheat the oven to 200°C (400°F), gas mark 6.

Peel the potatoes if you prefer, then cut into wedges.
Toss them in the oil, then the spice mixture, and
roast in the oven for about 40 minutes.

Sprinkle with sea salt and serve with sweet chilli
sauce as a dip.

Mega-maxi cheeseburger

Serves 4
Preparation time: 10 minutes
Cooking time: 10 minutes

4 large burgers from your butcher, each about 150 g (5 oz)
100 g (3½ oz) Gorgonzola or mascarpone cheese
4 sesame burger rolls
100 g (3½ oz) Cheddar cheese, cut into 4 slices
2 ripe tomatoes, finely sliced
tomato ketchup
pickled gherkins

Heat a frying pan or grill.

Grill or fry the burgers on one side, turn them over, then place slices of Gorgonzola or the mascarpone onto the cooked sides. Continue to cook until the cheese melts.

Toast the burger rolls. Place 1 slice of Cheddar cheese on the toasted base, then place with the cooked burger with the Gorgonzola or mascarpone on top.

Top with the tomato slices, ketchup, pickled gherkins and the remaining half of the burger roll and serve immediately.

Deep-fried whitebait

Just like baby vegetables, tiny fish hold a
fascination for children. My children take an
almost barbaric delight in swallowing these
little creatures whole, having first looked them
straight in the eye!

Serves 4
Preparation time: 5 minutes
Cooking time: 5 minutes

400 g (13 oz) whitebait (ready-prepared or rolled in
a little seasoned flour)
sea salt
freshly ground black pepper
lemon wedges

For the homemade ketchup:
oil for cooking
500 g (1 lb) tomatoes, skinned, deseeded and finely
chopped
250 g (8 oz) onions, finely chopped
500 g (1 lb) red peppers, deseeded and finely chopped
1 garlic clove, finely chopped
40 g (1½ oz) sugar
1 tablespoon Dijon mustard
1 teaspoon paprika
1 wineglass vinegar
a good pinch of ground cloves

To make the ketchup: heat the oil in a deep
saucepan and cook the tomatoes, onions, red
peppers and garlic for 45 minutes until very soft.

Pass the mixture through a sieve to remove all the
seeds. Return to the pan, add the remaining
ingredients and simmer for 1 hour.

Leave to cool, then transfer to a jar. The ketchup will
keep for 15 days in a refrigerator.

In a deep-fat fryer, or deep pan of hot oil, fry the
whitebait for about 3 minutes until golden (following
the supplier's instructions if they are frozen).

Season to taste and serve very hot with sea salt,
pepper, ketchup and lemon wedges.

Piperade

This simple version of the famous dish uses preserved Basque piquillos peppers, which can be found in good supermarkets or delicatessens. Failing that, just use 2 red, green or yellow peppers. If your children like spicy food, follow the Spanish example and add a good pinch of piment d'Espelette chilli flakes or chilli powder.

Serves 4
Preparation time: 10 minutes
Cooking time: 30 minutes

olive oil
5 large, ripe tomatoes, skinned and deseeded
1 red onion, finely chopped
400 g (13 oz) jar Basque piquillos peppers, drained and sliced
1 garlic clove, finely chopped
1 bay leaf
pinch of dried thyme
pinch of piment d'Espelette chilli flakes, or chilli powder (optional)
salt and freshly ground black pepper
1 teaspoon sugar
8 eggs
150 ml (¼ pint) single cream
4 large slices Bayonne or other cured ham

Heat a little oil in a large frying pan, then cook the vegetables together with the seasoning and sugar until very soft, almost reduced to a purée.

Beat the eggs with the cream. Then either stir the egg mixture into the vegetables and leave it to cook, or cook it in the traditional way for scrambled eggs. Fry the ham slices and serve with the piperade.

Chilli tortillas

Serves 4
Preparation time: 5 minutes

5 tortilla wraps
8 tablespoons Chilli con carne (see recipe opposite)
2 tomatoes, deseeded and finely diced
1 avocado, finely diced
1 teaspoon lemon juice

Heat the wraps in a dry frying pan. Fill with Chilli con carne, roll up and garnish with tomato and avocado, sprinkled with lemon juice to prevent discoloration.

Chilli con carne

The family dish par excellence. If you don't like spicy dishes, go easy on the chilli powder.

Serves 8
Preparation time: 15 minutes
Cooking time: 2 hours

The vegetables:
2 courgettes, coarsely chopped
2 large red peppers, coarsely chopped
1 yellow pepper, coarsely chopped
olive oil

The meat:
3 tablespoons olive oil
2 onions, chopped
2 carrots, chopped
1 tablespoon ground cumin
1 tablespoon dried oregano
4 garlic cloves, chopped
1.5 kg (2½ lb) minced beef
1 litre (1¾ pints) beef stock
1 small can tomato purée
400 g (14 oz) can chopped tomatoes
2 tablespoons good quality chilli powder
½ teaspoon Cayenne pepper
1 tablespoon sugar
1 teaspoon salt
2 teaspoons freshly ground black pepper
2 x 400 g (14 oz) cans red kidney beans, drained and rinsed
fresh parsley, chopped
crème fraîche

Quickly brown the vegetables in a little olive oil and set aside.

For the meat, heat the 3 tablespoons olive oil in a large casserole dish. Add the onions, carrots, cumin, oregano and garlic and cook over a moderate heat for 5 minutes. Turn up the heat and brown the meat. It is important that it fries quickly and browns well, so add it in batches, if necessary.

Add the stock, tomato purée, tomatoes, chilli powder, Cayenne pepper, sugar, salt and pepper. Mix well and leave to simmer without a lid for about 1 hour.

When the chilli has thickened, add the browned vegetables, kidney beans and parsley, cover and leave to cook for a further 10 minutes.

When almost ready to serve, add a spoonful of crème fraîche. Serve with hot tortilla wraps, crème fraîche, salad and grated Cheddar cheese.

Posh ham and mash

Serves 4
Preparation time: 10 minutes
Cooking time: 25 minutes

500 g (1 lb) potatoes, peeled and cut into pieces
1 litre (1¾ pints) full-fat milk
150 ml (¼ pint) single cream or crème fraîche
40 g (1½ oz) good quality butter
sea salt and freshly ground black pepper
4 egg yolks
4 large slices ham on the bone from your local
delicatessen

Poach the potatoes in the milk. Drain, add the
cream and butter and season to taste.

Using a hand potato-masher, mash the potatoes.

Spoon a mound of mashed potato onto each plate.
Make a well in the centre and top with an egg yolk.
Roll up the slice of ham and serve alongside the
mashed potato.

Koftas with charmoula

Serves 4
Preparation time: 20 minutes
Cooking time: 10 minutes

400 g (14 oz) minced beef or lamb
1 teaspoon ground cumin
2 small onions, chopped
salt and freshly ground black pepper
1 tablespoon olive oil

For the charmoula:
1 tablespoon chopped coriander
1 tablespoon chopped flat leaf parsley
1 garlic clove, very finely chopped
1 tablespoon candied lemon peel, very finely chopped
2 tablespoons olive oil
sea salt and freshly ground black pepper

Combine the meat with the cumin and onions. Season well with salt and pepper. With your hands, shape the mixture into small balls and fry in hot oil until golden.

Combine all the charmoula ingredients and serve with the meat.

Saddle of rabbit with Boursin cheese

Serves 4
Preparation time: 5 minutes
Cooking time: 1 hour

2 shallots, finely chopped
olive oil
4 saddles of rabbit
150 ml (¼ pint) white wine
salt and freshly ground black pepper
75 g (3 oz) Boursin cheese
100 ml (3½ fl oz) single cream

Preheat the oven to 180°C (350°F), gas mark 4.

In a flame-proof casserole dish, brown the shallots in the oil, then fry the rabbit until golden all over. Moisten with the wine, add salt and pepper to taste and sufficient water to cover the rabbit, then bring to the boil.

Place in the oven and cook for about 1 hour.

Remove from the oven and melt the Boursin into the cooking juices. Add the cream, season to taste, and serve with pasta.

Roast pork with celeriac and apple mash and cranberry sauce

Serves 6
Preparation time: 15 minutes
Cooking time: 1¼ hours

1 good quality pork joint (e.g. loin) from your butcher, about 1 kg (2 lb) in weight
olive oil
sea salt and freshly ground black pepper
1 celeriac
4 cooking apples
150ml (¼ pint) crème fraîche
40 g (1½ oz) unsalted butter
300 g (10 oz) fresh cranberries
3 tablespoons caster sugar

Preheat the oven to 180°C (350°F), gas mark 4.

Brush the pork joint with oil and season with salt and pepper. Place in a roasting tin and roast in the oven for about 1¼ hours, basting the meat frequently.

When the meat is cooked, remove from the oven and leave to rest for 10 minutes before carving.

While the meat is cooking, peel the celeriac, cut into pieces, and cook in salted boiling water for about 20 minutes.

Peel the apples, cut into pieces, and add for the last few minutes of the cooking time.

Drain, add the crème fraîche and butter, then mash until smooth.

Poach the cranberries in a little hot water until they are very soft. Add the sugar and continue to cook until dissolved.

Carve the pork into slices and serve with the mash and cranberry sauce.

Too-good-to-be true pork ribs

In the same way as Chilli tortillas (see page 20), this fun dish eaten with the fingers, is perfect for grown-ups and children alike.

Serves 6
Preparation time: 20 minutes
Marinating time: 4–5 hours
Cooking time: 2 hours

1.5 kg (3 lb) rib joint of pork

For the marinade:
2 shallots, finely chopped
1 garlic clove
3 tablespoons rice wine vinegar
2 tablespoons olive oil
5 tablespoons Hoi sin sauce (Chinese barbecue sauce, available in the cooking sauces section of your supermarket)
4 tablespoons water
1 tablespoon soy sauce
freshly ground white pepper
½ red chilli, finely chopped (optional)

Prepare the marinade in a roasting dish by mixing together all the ingredients.

Coat the ribs on all sides, cover the dish with clingfilm and leave to marinate in a cool place for 4–5 hours, turning from time to time.

Preheat the oven to 140°C (275°F), gas mark 1.

Roast the ribs for 2–2½ hours, turning occasionally if you remember. Serve with rice and a whole pile of paper napkins!

Cordon bleu cordon bleu

If you prefer, this dish can be made with chicken breasts sliced through horizontally, opened out and flattened

Serves 4
Preparation time: 10 minutes
Cooking time: 5 minutes

4 milk-reared veal escalopes, or chicken breasts
3–4 tablespoons flour, seasoned with a pinch of sea salt and some freshly ground black pepper and sprinkled onto a plate
50 g (2 oz) unsalted butter
2–3 tablespoons olive oil
100 g (3½ oz) freshly grated Parmesan cheese
handful sundried tomatoes
sea salt, freshly ground black pepper
1 lemon

On a chopping board, spread out one escalope, or slit open one chicken breast horizontally and open out. Cover with clingfilm.

Using a meat tenderizer (or a rolling pin) and with the help of the younger diners (they love this part), flatten the chicken breasts as much as possible. Repeat the procedure with the remaining escalopes or fillets.

Coat both sides of the veal or chicken in the seasoned flour, pressing down firmly to ensure the flour adheres well.

Heat a frying pan and add a knob of butter and a little olive oil. When the butter 'sizzles' (get the little cherubs to listen), add 1 or 2 escalopes and brown for several minutes.

Turn the escalope over, then place the Parmesan and the tomatoes on the golden side. Fold the escalope in half and continue to cook, pressing down on the meat so that the Parmesan melts.

Turn the escalope over once again, if necessary.

Season to taste and serve immediately with a little lemon juice.

Marie's sautéed veal with optional olives

This perfect weekend dish goes down well with everyone, fills the kitchen with wonderful aromas and leaves you with hours of quality time to spend with your children.

Serves 6
Preparation time: 10 minutes
Cooking time: 1½ hours

2 tablespoons olive oil
3 shallots, finely chopped
3 carrots, sliced
1 kg (2 lb) shoulder of veal, diced
1 litre (1¾ pints) water
salt and freshly ground pepper
200 g (7 oz) jar pitted green olives, drained

Preheat the oven to 180°C (350°F), gas mark 4.

In a cast-iron casserole dish, heat the oil, then brown the shallots and carrots. Add the meat and fry until golden on all sides.

Add the measured water to the casserole dish and stir well to mix all the ingredients. Add a little salt and pepper, then bring to the boil. Place the casserole dish in the oven and cook for about 1½ hours.

Add the olives. Serve with olive oil mashed potato or polenta, and don't get worked up if the children leave half the olives on the sides of their plates.

Roast beef with sweet potato chips

Serves 6
Preparation time: 10 minutes
Cooking time: 40 minutes

1 top quality beef joint, about 1 kg (2 lb) in weight
olive oil
875 g (1¾ lb) sweet potatoes, peeled and cut into chips
sea salt and freshly ground black pepper

Preheat the oven to 200°C (400°F), gas mark 6.

Place the meat in an ovenproof dish and brush
with olive oil. Put in the oven and cook for 25–30
minutes. Keep an eye on the meat unless you know
your oven very well, as it can get overcooked.

Remove the meat from the oven and leave to rest
for 10–15 minutes.

Meanwhile, heat 2–3 tablespoons oil in a frying
pan and fry the sweet potatoes for 4–5 minutes
until beautifully golden. Drain on kitchen paper,
season with salt and pepper and serve with slices
of roast beef.

Real bolognaise sauce

Serves 4–6
Preparation time: 15 minutes
Cooking time: 1½ hours

20 g (¾ oz) unsalted butter
150 g (5 oz) streaky bacon, diced or cut into small pieces
2 onions, finely chopped
2 carrots, sliced
2 celery sticks, diced
1 garlic clove, crushed
500 g (1 lb) minced beef
250 g (8 oz) tomato passata
400 g (14 oz) can tomatoes
100 ml (3½ fl oz) red wine
100 ml (3½ fl oz) beef stock
salt and freshly ground black pepper

Melt the butter in a large sauté pan and fry the
bacon, onions, carrots, celery and garlic. When the
vegetables are soft and slightly golden, increase the
heat and brown the meat, adding a little at a time.

Pour in the passata, canned tomatoes, wine
and stock. Season to taste and leave to simmer,
uncovered, for about 1 hour until the sauce is very
thick, adding a little more stock if it becomes too dry.

Serve with pasta and freshly grated Parmesan
cheese.

Spicy beef, hummus, pine nuts and multi-coloured baby courgettes

Adapted from a dish served at the Moro restaurant in London, this mixture of flavours, textures and colours is a hit with my children. It has been included in this chapter as you may have difficulty finding the multi-coloured baby courgettes at your local shop and need to go to a big supermarket.

Serves 4
Preparation time: 5 minutes
Cooking time: 10 minutes

2 tablespoons olive oil
1 garlic clove, finely chopped
2 shallots, finely chopped
500 g (1 lb) top-quality minced beef
1 teaspoon ground cumin
1 teaspoon ground nutmeg
salt and freshly ground black pepper
dozen baby courgettes in a variety of colours, partially peeled
4 tablespoons hummus
dozen cherry tomatoes, cut in quarters
30 g (1 oz) pine nuts
few sprigs of fresh coriander

Heat the oil in a frying pan and brown the garlic and shallots. Add the beef, breaking it up as much as possible against the base of the pan. Fry the meat over a high heat until it is crispy. When cooked, add the cumin and nutmeg, and season with salt and pepper. Stir well, then set aside.

Cook the courgettes for just a few minutes in salted boiling water, then drain.

Combine the courgettes with the quartered tomatoes, spoon onto plates, top with the beef mixture, a tablespoon of hummus and a sprinkling of pine nuts and coriander leaves.

Irish stew

One of Ireland's national dishes: lamb simply baked in a slow oven with potatoes, onions, parsley and thyme. The luxury version includes carrots and sometimes even leeks.

Serves 4–6
Preparation time: 10 minutes
Cooking time: 2 hours

500 g (1 lb) firm potatoes, finely sliced
750 g (1½ lb) stewing lamb
2 onions, finely sliced
1 tablespoon chopped parsley
1 tablespoon fresh thyme
300 ml (½ pint) water
salt and freshly ground black pepper

Preheat the oven to 160°C (325°F), gas mark 3.

Place alternate layers of potato, lamb, onions and herbs in a casserole dish, finishing with a layer of potatoes, and press gently to pack all the ingredients together in the casserole. Add the measured water and season with salt and pepper.

Cover and bake in the preheated oven for about 2 hours or until the meat is tender.

Red onion tortilla

Serves 4
Preparation time: 10 minutes
Cooking time: 30 minutes

2 tablespoons olive oil
2 red onions, chopped
500 g (1 lb) potatoes, cooked and sliced
6 eggs
100 ml (3½ fl oz) single cream
sea salt and freshly ground black pepper

Heat the oil in a frying pan and fry the onions until soft. Add the potatoes and cook for a few more minutes, ensuring that the slices do not break up.

Beat the eggs together with the cream, pour into the frying pan, season with salt and pepper and cook over a very low heat.

Turn the tortilla out onto a plate and serve warm.

Marmalade-glazed duck

Serves 6–8
Preparation time: 5 minutes
Cooking time: 1 hour

1 large duck
3 tablespoons orange marmalade
1 tablespoon olive oil
sea salt

Preheat the oven to 190°C (375°F), gas mark 5.

If possible, take the duck out of the refrigerator 30 minutes before putting it in the oven.

In a bowl, combine 2 tablespoons of the marmalade with the olive oil and a little sea salt.

Place the duck on a rack in a roasting tin and roast in the oven for 30 minutes. Remove the duck from the oven, drain off the fat, brush the duck with the oil-and-marmalade mixture and return it to the oven to cook for a further 30 minutes.

When cooked, remove the duck from the roasting tin, collecting all the juices from inside the cavity. Leave the duck to rest for a few minutes on a chopping board.

Remove as much of the fat as possible, then add the remaining marmalade to the roasting tin and de-glaze, scraping off all the sticky deposits.

Serve with basmati rice and Chinese crackers.

Glazed salmon

Serves 4
Preparation time: 10 minutes
Cooking time: 5–8 minutes

2 tablespoons clear honey
1 tablespoon olive oil
1 tablespoon soy sauce
4 salmon steaks, skin removed

Combine the honey, oil and soy sauce and brush over the salmon.

Place the salmon steaks on an ovenproof baking sheet and grill for 5–8 minutes until they are beautifully golden.

Serve with basmati rice or coconut-milk crushed, or lightly mashed potatoes.

Chicken korma

A good way of introducing the flavour of spices.
I have deliberately omitted the chilli from this
recipe and suggested serving the garnishes
separately to avoid taking any chances.

Serves 4
Preparation time: 15 minutes
Cooking time: 30–35 minutes

For the spice paste:
1 onion, finely chopped
2 garlic cloves
½ teaspoon turmeric
½ teaspoon ground cumin
½ teaspoon ground cardamom
½ teaspoon ground cinnamon
½ teaspoon coriander seeds
thumb-sized piece of fresh ginger
50 g (2 oz) cashew nuts

2 tablespoons olive oil
4 chicken breast fillets, cut into bite-sized pieces
400 ml (14 fl oz) coconut milk

To garnish:
a selection of fresh coriander, raisins, blanched almonds
and cashew nuts, and diced fresh mango

Combine all the ingredients for the spice paste in
a blender or food mixer.

Heat the oil in a frying pan and fry the paste over
a low heat for 3–4 minutes.

Add the chicken pieces and brown for no longer
than 4–5 minutes.

Add the coconut milk to the frying pan together
with a little water, stir well and leave to simmer for
15 minutes.

Serve with basmati rice, naan bread and the
garnishes in small bowls.

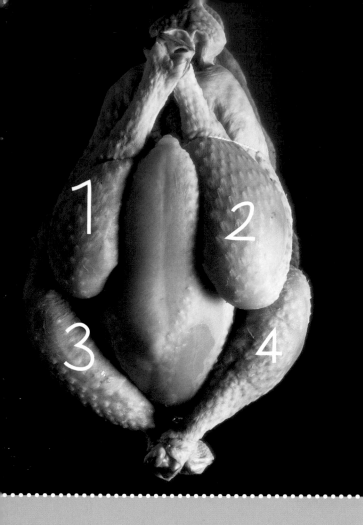

Citrus-glazed chicken

Serves 4
Preparation time: 5 minutes
Cooking time: 10 minutes

2 tablespoons olive oil
1 shallot, very finely chopped
4 skinless chicken breasts, sliced
2 tablespoons soy sauce
2 tablespoons clear honey
juice of 1 orange and 1 lemon
sea salt and freshly ground black pepper

Heat the oil in a frying pan and gently fry the shallot and then the chicken pieces.

Mix together the soy sauce, honey, and orange and lemon juice, heating gently to combine the honey, if necessary.

Pour the sauce over the chicken and cook for 7–8 minutes. The cooking juices will reduce to form a delicious glaze over the chicken.

Serve with basmati rice.

Four-legged chicken

A close relation of the five-legged sheep, this beast will help you overcome the perennial problem of what to do when the number of guests exceeds the number of legs available (when the chicken is carved.)

Cook exactly as you would an ordinary chicken. The trickiest thing is to find a butcher that won't take you for a half-wit when you ask him to prepare the bird.

I have some addresses if you need them!

Corn on the cob

OK, nine times out of ten, home-cooked corncobs come frozen and are cooked in the microwave. So saying, they really are better fresh, while in season, served with lashings of butter.

Serves 4
Preparation time: 3 minutes
Cooking time: 5 minutes

4 corncobs
lashings of good quality butter
salt and pepper
umpteen paper napkins
4 toothbrushes for cleaning teeth after eating

Plunge the corncobs into a large pan of salted boiling water.

Cook for 4–5 minutes, (check a kernel with a sharp skewer) then leave to cool for a few minutes before serving with the butter and salt and pepper.

Homemade desserts

Let good sensible eating prevail during the week (as my favourite paediatrician Dr V advises), but come the weekend, or when there is a special occasion, let's have a treat. I like to take extra care over the meal from start to finish at these times.

Here's my Sugababes (I mean my kids) current Top Ten.

Lemon and raspberry tart

A pretty dessert that children can make all on their own from the age of seven or eight.

Serves 4
Preparation time: 10 minutes
Chilling time: 1 hour

10–15 shortbread biscuits
50 g (2 oz) butter, melted
1 jar lemon curd
250 g (8 oz) fresh raspberries
icing sugar

Crush the shortbread biscuits and combine with the melted butter in a large mixing bowl.

Press the biscuit crumbs into the base of 4 rings (or pastry cutters, or even bun tins) and leave to set in the refrigerator for about 1 hour.

Turn the shortbread mixture out, spread each base with lemon curd (depth, to suit!) and decorate with the raspberries and a dusting of icing sugar.

Five-finger cake

Very simple to make, with no cooking involved, and lots of stages that your children can help with. Take full advantage of the food marketing men and women's efforts by using these little biscuits. They should be encouraged and supported each time they abstain from stupidly palming us off with cartoon characters on fish finger packets or yogurt pots to indicate that the food is for children.

Serves 8–10
Preparation time: 20 minutes
Chilling time: 2 hours

1 packet of each variety of chocolate finger biscuits (caramel, giant, mini, plain, milk and white chocolate, or whatever combination you like)
50 g (2 oz) butter, you may need a little more depending on the absorbency of the biscuit crumbs
200 ml (7 fl oz) whipping cream
400 g (14 oz) good-quality dark chocolate

You will need a loose-based square or rectangular baking tin.

Crush the chocolate finger biscuits (between 500 g and 750 g, (1 to 1½ lb), depending on the size of your baking tin), reserving enough whole biscuits of each variety for the decoration.

Melt the butter and combine well with the biscuit crumbs. Press the mixture into the base of the baking tin with the fingertips and place in a refrigerator to set.

Bring the cream just to the boil. Add the chocolate to the cream, then stir until it has completely melted and the cream mixture is smooth and glossy.

Pour over the chilled biscuit base and leave to set in a refrigerator for several hours.

Dip the tin for a few seconds in hot water to ease the decanting of the cake.

Turn the cake out of the baking tin and decorate with the reserved chocolate fingers, softening the chocolate base of each biscuit, momentarily, to make them stick firmly.

Baked apples with chocolate toffee

Serves 4
Preparation time: 10 minutes
Cooking time: 25 minutes

2 or 3 Dime bars or similar chocolate coated hard toffee
4 large cooking apples, well cored but not quite through
125 g (4 oz) plain flour
50 g (2 oz) sugar
75 g (3 oz) unsalted butter

Preheat the oven to 180°C (350°F), gas mark 4. Put the Dime bars in a tea cloth and bash them to small pieces with a rolling pin. Children like this bit!

Rub the butter into the flour and sugar until the mixture resembles fine breadcrumbs. Stir in the toffee pieces and spoon into the apple cavities. Cut through the skin around each apple's waist, to prevent it from bursting.

Place in a baking tin, cover with kitchen foil and bake for 15 minutes. Remove the foil and bake for a further 10–15 minutes.

Remove from oven, leave to cool slightly (in case the melted toffee burns tiny tongues!) and serve with vanilla ice cream or crème fraîche.

Pancakes

There's nothing great about making pancakes for six in a smoke-filled kitchen. The production line never runs smoothly and the pancake-maker (me!) is always left short-tempered and hungry.

I have managed to get round this problem with a multi-hyper-nice-but-don't-touch-my-pancake-that's-mine-on-the-left machine. I have no difficulty imposing eggs, ham, tomatoes, cheese and salmon fillings before the sugary avalanche: children are much more motivated when they cook the pancakes themselves.

If you don't fancy Frodo-size pancakes, you can treat yourself to a little session on your own beforehand with a normal sized pancake pan. They keep and reheat very well.

Serves 4
Preparation time: 2 minutes
Resting time: 30 minutes

150 g (5 oz) plain flour
3 eggs
750 ml (1¼ pints) milk
50 g (2 oz) butter, melted

Place the flour in a large mixing bowl. Make a well in the centre, add the eggs and combine with the flour to produce a reasonably thick paste. Gradually add the cold milk and melted butter, beating hard to avoid lumps.

If you like your pancakes light, leave the mixture to rest for 30 minutes.

Pancake gâteau

A sort of buttery cake made of pancakes. This recipe also works well with shop-bought packets of pancakes, as long as you avoid the flavoured ones, which are often too strong.

Serves 6–8

about 20 pancakes
150 g (5 oz) butter
4–5 tablespoons sugar
juice and rind of 2 lemons

Preheat the oven to 150°C (300°F), gas mark 2.

To assemble the cake, spread a little butter over each pancake, dredge with sugar and sprinkle with a little lemon juice, then stack the pancakes one on top of the other.

Bake in the preheated oven for a few minutes before serving.

Poached apricots with toasted Madeira cake and Greek yogurt

Serves 4
Preparation time: 20 minutes
Cooking time: 10 minutes

about 10 fresh apricots, pitted and halved
juice of 2 oranges
1 vanilla pod, split
2 tablespoons granulated sugar
4 slices Madeira cake (see page 140)
1 small pot of Greek yogurt
2 or 3 thin slices unwaxed, or well-scrubbed orange,
to decorate

In a large saucepan, poach the apricots with the orange juice, vanilla pod and sugar, adding a little water if necessary. Leave to cool.

Toast the slices of Madeira cake, taking care not to set your toaster alight – it's best to toast them under the grill. Place 1 slice on each plate, spoon the stewed apricots on top, decorate with the orange slices and serve with the yogurt.

Raspberry jam tart

With homemade jam and pastry, if you please.

Serves 6–8
Preparation time: 20 minutes
Resting time: 2 hours
Cooking time: 30 minutes

250 g (8 oz) flour
125 g (4 oz) butter, very cold and cut into small pieces
3 tablespoons water, very cold
500 g (1 lb) raspberry jam

Sift the flour into a large mixing bowl, add the butter and rub in with the fingertips until the mixture resembles fine breadcrumbs. Add enough water to mix to a firm dough and shape the mixture into a ball.

Wrap the pastry in clingfilm and place in a refrigerator for 2 hours.

Preheat the oven to 180°C (350°F), gas mark 4.

Roll out the pastry and use to line a 28-cm (11-inch) tart plate. Prick over the base with a fork and bake in the preheated oven for about 10 minutes.

Remove the tart case from the oven, spread with the jam and bake for a further 20 minutes. Leave to cool slightly (watch out, hot jam can burn tiny tongues!) before serving with vanilla ice cream or crème fraîche.

Red berry fruit trifle

An excellent recipe to make with children that teaches them how the textures and tastes of foods can change depending on cooking temperature and time.

Serves 4
Preparation time: 10 minutes
Cooking time: 15 minutes
Chilling time: several hours

125 g (4 oz) raspberries
2 tablespoons sugar
125 g (4 oz) cherries, pitted and halved
handful dried red berry fruits, such as cranberries
125 g (4 oz) strawberries, sliced
1 egg yolk
4 tablespoons mascarpone cheese
4 slices sponge cake, or trifle sponges
1 pomegranate

In a large saucepan, cook the raspberries together with 1 tablespoon of the sugar over a low heat for a few minutes. Add the cherries and the dried fruits, then leave to simmer until the cherries are soft and the dried fruits have absorbed the cooking juices. Remove from the heat and add the strawberries, which will cook through in the hot compote.

Add a little more sugar, if necessary, and leave to cool completely.

Beat the egg yolk with the remaining sugar until the mixture is thick and pale, then fold into the mascarpone cheese.

Place a sponge cake slice or trifle sponge in the bottom of each glass or dessert bowl.

Pour over the fruit mixture and top with the mascarpone mixture.

Leave to chill in a refrigerator for several hours before serving.

Yogurt and honey ice cream with olive oil pancakes

You will need an ice cream maker to make this recipe. Do not resort to using forks and Tupperware containers in the freezer.

Serves 6
Preparation time: 25 minutes

500 ml (17 fl oz) custard, much better if homemade (see page 60)
500 g (1 lb) Greek yogurt
6 sweet olive oil pancakes (available from delicatessens and some supermarkets)
3–4 tablespoons clear honey

Pour the custard and the yogurt into the ice cream maker. When the ice cream has set, scoop balls of ice cream onto the pancakes and drizzle with the honey.

Knickerbocker Glory with cherries, strawberries and bananas

Serves 4
Preparation time: 20 minutes
Cooking time: 10 minutes

300 g (10 oz) cherries, pitted
2–3 tablespoons sugar
150 ml (¼ pint) whipping cream
1 tablespoon mascarpone cheese
500 g (1 lb) vanilla ice cream
250 g (8 oz) strawberries, finely sliced
2 bananas, finely sliced and sprinkled with a little lemon juice to prevent discoloration

Set aside a few cherries for decoration. Place the remaining cherries in a large saucepan with the sugar and cook gently to produce a compote. Purée in a blender to produce a smooth sauce, then leave to cool completely.

Whip the cream and mascarpone into stiff peaks.

Build up the Knickerbocker Glory with alternate layers of ice cream, mascarpone-cream mixture, strawberries and bananas, then pour over the fruit sauce. Decorate with the reserved cherries and serve immediately.

Fresh mango served with raspberry sauce

Serves 4
Preparation time: 10 minutes

2 mangoes, perfectly ripe
150 g (5 oz) raspberries
2–3 tablespoons icing sugar

Cut the mangoes in half lengthways, avoiding the stone in the middle. Cut the flesh in a criss-cross pattern inside the fruit, then carefully turn the flesh towards the outside, taking care not to break the skin of the fruit, to give a pretty 'hedgehog' effect.

Heat the raspberries in a large saucepan and cook until they form a coulis. Pass through a sieve to remove the pips. Add icing sugar to taste, depending on the acidity of the raspberries. Leave to cool and serve with the mango.

Lemon meringue ice cream gâteau

Serves 10
Preparation time: 20 minutes
Chilling time: 3 hours

400 ml (14 fl oz) whipping cream
3 tablespoons mascarpone cheese
4 tablespoons icing sugar
juice and rind of 4 lemons
2 packets small meringues
6 tablespoons lemon curd

Using a blender or a hand-held electric mixer, whip up the cream, mascarpone and sugar. Fold in the lemon juice and grated rind and 1 packet of the meringues, coarsely crumbled.

Using a metal tablespoon, fold in the lemon curd, trying not to incorporate it too much, but rather to leave ripples in the mixture.

Pour the mixture into a flexible silicon loaf tin or a freezer-proof container lined with clingfilm, leaving enough hanging over the edges to use as handles when unmoulding the gâteau.

Leave in the freezer for about 3 hours until set. Turn out onto a serving plate and decorate with the remaining meringues.

Homemade ice cream

2-in-1 ice creams for 3–4 year olds

In France it verges on gastronomic blasphemy to imitate recipes of a commercial ice cream manufacturer by using a mixture of bought cakes and a good quality vanilla ice cream.

From my own personal experience, limited as it may be, I believe that it's important not to set excessively high standards for very young children. Otherwise, the experience is soon turned into a lesson, as though they were at school. After all, at four years of age, there are not really many techniques they can master on their own in the kitchen.

Just get a tub of vanilla ice cream, a selection of cakes, desserts and toppings and let their imaginations run riot.

Children are enchanted with the idea of splashing about with the melting ice cream, breaking the cakes up into pieces, mixing everything together like a potion and then transforming the mixture as though by magic in the freezer. They quickly and easily manage to make gourmet desserts, of which they are extremely proud.

If you simply cannot bear the sight of fresh new cakes being smashed to pieces, or if you insist on everything being homemade, then use the leftovers from homemade desserts and make your own vanilla ice cream using the Custard recipe opposite.

Combination ideas

Lemon, apple or pear tart, all sorts of crumbles, macaroons, brownies, cookies, cheesecakes, chocolate bars, preserves, chocolate spread, Nutella chocolate and hazelnut spread… the list is endless.

Armelle's custard

Tricky the first time round, but once you master the technique this is a delicious treat that everyone will enjoy. Armelle's recipe is so good that she serves it in stemmed glasses as a dessert in its own right!

Preparation time: 10 minutes
Cooking time: 10 minutes

250 ml (8 fl oz) full-fat milk
250 ml (8 fl oz) single cream
1 or 2 vanilla pods
6 egg yolks
150 g (5 oz) caster sugar

Split the vanilla pods and scrape the seeds into a large saucepan together with the milk and cream. Bring to the boil. Meanwhile, beat the egg yolks with the sugar until the mixture becomes pale and frothy and has doubled in volume. Pour the hot milk-and-cream mixture over the eggs, stirring vigorously. Return the mixture to the pan and heat, stirring continuously with a wooden spoon. Taking care that it does not come to the boil, cook the custard mixture until it thickens.

The custard is cooked when your finger leaves a mark in the mixture on the back of the spoon.

It is vital to remove from the heat as soon as the custard is ready.

As it continues to cook even when taken off the heat and as the base of the pan always cooks more quickly than the rest, I always pour the custard into another container, chilled if possible, leaving behind the remains at the base of the saucepan.

If you are unfortunate enough to discover lumps in your nice custard, beat extremely vigorously with a wooden spoon to make them disappear.

plenty of time

Meringue glacé

Here's the next stage on. It requires a mould and a little dexterity, as you've got to move quite quickly. It's perfect for six-to seven-year olds.

Serves 8–10 (in theory, but my 4 children wolfed down the one in the photo in one fell swoop)
Preparation time: 10 minutes
Chilling time: 2 hours

500 ml (17 fl oz) lime sorbet
500 ml (17 fl oz) mango sorbet
500 ml (17 fl oz) coconut sorbet
3 packets small meringues, crushed, reserving a few whole ones for the decoration

You will need a loose-based flexible silicon baking tin.

Remove the sorbets from the freezer 20 minutes before you start to make the gâteau.

Start with a layer of crushed meringues, then assemble alternate layers of sorbet and meringue. Decorate with whole meringues and sprinkle over a few meringues crushed into a powder.

Place in a freezer for about 2 hours.

For maximum gourmet effect, top with a mound of whipped cream just before serving.

Mango and pineapple cappuccino

Serves 4
Preparation time: 10 minutes

4 pieces frozen or canned mango*
8 tablespoons frozen or canned pineapple chunks*
juice of 2 limes
200 ml (7 fl oz) whipping cream
1 tablespoon mascarpone cheese
1–2 tablespoons sugar
4 scoops coconut sorbet

Leave the mango and pineapple to defrost slightly, then, while still slightly frozen, blend them in a liquidizer together with the lime juice and reduce them to a purée. Pour into glasses.

*If you are using canned fruit, drain first, and you may not need so much lime juice.

Whip together the cream, mascarpone and sugar, then spoon a thick layer over the fruit purée.

Hide the scoops of sorbet in the whipped mascarpone cream and serve immediately.

Caramel and apple sundae

Serves 4
Preparation time: 2 minutes

2 jars or cans stewed apple with no added sugar, or prepare your own
2–3 Dime bars, broken into pieces (see page 48)
4 scoops vanilla ice cream

Spoon the stewed apple into the glasses.

Add a layer of Dime bar pieces, then top with a scoop of ice cream.

You can also add caramel or butterscotch sauce.

Apricot and popcorn sundae

Serves 4
Preparation time: 3 minutes

4 tablespoons canned or fresh apricot halves
2 tablespoons sugar
vanilla or white chocolate ice cream
favourite sauce (raspberry, strawberry, caramel,
chocolate…)
popcorn

If using fresh apricots, heat them with the sugar in
a saucepan and cook until just soft. The fruits must
retain their shape. Leave to cool.

Spoon the stewed apricots into glass bowls, add
the vanilla ice cream, pour over the sauce, and
sprinkle with popcorn.

Double choc sundae

Serves 4
Preparation time: 2 minutes

4 scoops chocolate ice cream
4 scoops vanilla ice cream
4 chocolate-covered meringues

Simply place scoops of the ice cream in sundae
dishes or small glasses, and top with a meringue.

Why not finish off with a hot chocolate fudge sauce
made by melting 100 g (3½ oz) dark chocolate with
20 g (¾ oz) unsalted butter and 1 tablespoon of
water?

No time at all

Now it's official – we have 36 minutes to make the evening meal and, here in France at least, often even less for lunch if the children come home at midday. Equally official are the statistics relating to children's health problems due to their diet. The culprits are excess sugar and salt, lack of physical activity and not eating enough fruit and vegetables.

Due to lack of time, we are often tempted to reach for the packs of ready-made meals in the fridge or the freezer, pierce the film three times and pop it in the microwave. Equally tempting are the desserts and cheeses decorated with pictures of cartoon characters. But all too often it's precisely these types of products that contain too much sugar and salt and too many additives, colourings and preservatives.

Seven tips from the experts

1 As often as possible, try to replace chocolate-flavour cereals with oat flakes or 'neutral' cereals (such as Weetabix or Rice Krispies) and muesli mixtures with no added sugar.

2 At breakfast, give the children lots of milk and some fruit juice(s) to drink. Stick with water at other mealtimes. Leave squashes and fizzy drinks for 'special occasions'.

3 Cut down on their crisp consumption. Don't provide them automatically when it comes to picnics and don't give them as a regular teatime snack when they get home from school.

4 Don't feel obliged to serve a 'real' pudding with each meal. Give them fruit or a yogurt and keep the homemade desserts or pots of mousse, caramel custard and other creamy chocolate desserts for special treats.

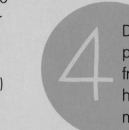

5 Don't feel guilty if the vegetables and fruits are not freshly picked from your kitchen garden or bought from the market that morning. Take advantage of the time you will gain by using ready-prepared frozen vegetables. And remember, canned vegetables are better than no vegetables at all!

6 Put the fast-food restaurants in their place. It's not a matter of banning fast foods totally: they too are part of a child's voyage of discovery through the world of tastes. Personally, I only resort to fast foods when it suits me (kitchen out of service, empty fridge before or after a journey). There is no longer any idea of it being a 'big occasion' – the place to celebrate them is at a real 'grown-ups' restaurant'.

7 To abide by the rule – which seems almost impossible to me – of 5 portions of fruit and vegetables per day, just say that one 'portion' corresponds to the amount the child can hold in one hand – and things will be better already. It only takes a freshly squeezed fruit juice in the morning, a piece of fruit when they get home from school and at lunchtime, or with the evening meal, a vegetable both at lunchtime and with the evening meal, and you've achieved your quota.

My cupboard survival kit comprises pasta, rice, polenta, semolina, and a few cans of chopped tomatoes, sweetcorn, lentils and chickpeas, while not forgetting a good stock of dried fruits (apricots, pears, prunes and dates). In the fridge, there is always a good quality Parmesan (Parmigiano Reggiano) or Cheddar cheese, some organic smoked fish, some hummus, preserved tomatoes, cream, eggs, bacon and a little good quality dry cured ham.

Here in France, I'm lucky enough to live two doors away from a supermarket filled with English, Lebanese and Japanese foods, which also has wonderful fish, fruit and vegetable counters. As it's open from 8.30 am to 9.00 pm, I consider my beloved local supermarket an extension of my fridge and cupboards. No longer do I suffer the distress of the forgotten item, as I did when I lived in the country and could only do one 'big shop' a week.

With a wonderful, thrice weekly market just a short walk away and a wide choice of top-quality shops just a little bit further, I'm spoilt for choice. Shopping for 'fresh' foods is no longer the constraint it once was. But my cupboard and freezer basics have not changed.

I'm a great fan of some frozen foods. When I was pregnant, I often wolfed down extremely flavoursome exotic ready-prepared meals, which quickly satisfied my cravings for, sometimes extremely odd, combinations, such as onion quiche served with chicken tikka sauce. Feeding the babies who have now grown so big is a much more serious matter and, except in an absolute emergency, these dishes now leave me colder than the inside of the white chests in which we find them.

One minor detail that will promote the cause of taste: take care when seasoning dishes. Treat yourself to good quality sea salt, whole peppercorns, a 'chic' olive oil, top quality butter, fresh untreated lemons and some quality crème fraîche. These small investments will make all the difference and will stimulate little taste buds.

On the other hand, I freeze my fingertips – with great pleasure and a clear conscience – filling my freezer with fantastic ingredients, ready-prepared to save time. Foods such as roasted vegetables, organic peas, tomatoes cut into quarters, peeled broad beans and mushrooms, slices of mango, citrus fruit quarters, small loins of lamb, carpaccio and fish steaks. I would happily hug the person who had the brilliant idea of putting cooked rice (two varieties!) and wheat in a bag.

Survival kit

Eggy Toast

As a child in my family, this used to be the dish for convalescents. If the plate was cleared in the evening, I would definitely be putting on my school uniform the next morning! It's a good way of getting children to eat eggs and milk. Always keep some sliced bread in the freezer and play around with pastry cutters to create fun shapes.

Serves 4
Preparation time: 3 minutes
Cooking time: 5 minutes

2 eggs
200 ml (7 fl oz) full-fat milk
30 g (1 oz) unsalted butter
4–5 slices bread (white, but not necessarily!)
a little sugar

Lightly beat the eggs with the milk.

Melt the butter in a frying pan. Quickly soak the pieces of bread in the egg-and-milk mixture, squeeze out any excess and fry until golden.

Sprinkle with a little sugar and serve very hot.

Chic cheese on toast

No need to get out the fondue set. The marketing people have kindly lined up small quantities of ready-sliced raclette and other cheeses in plastic wrappers that keep for a long time in the fridge, so why not use them.

Serves 4
Preparation time: 5 minutes
Cooking time: 3 minutes

4 small potatoes, cooked in boiling water and sliced
8–10 slices good quality dry cured ham
250 g (8 oz) raclette or other melting cheese, sliced
4 slices country-style bread
a few lettuce leaves
pickled gherkins or cherry tomatoes

Place the slices of hot potato and the ham on the bread and top with the cheese slices.

Grill for 2–3 minutes until the cheese has thoroughly melted. Serve with the lettuce and pickled gherkins.

Cheese + Sweetcorn Toasties

Serves 4
Preparation time: 5 minutes
Cooking time: 3 minutes

1 can sweetcorn
250 g (8 oz) good quality farmhouse Cheddar cheese, grated
4 slices white or country-style bread
50 g (2 oz) butter

Drain the sweetcorn and combine with the grated cheese. Spread on top of the bread and place under a hot grill for 3 minutes until the cheese has melted and browned slightly.

Serve with a knob of butter.

71

Pasta with prawns, garlic and tomatoes

Serves 4
Cooking time: 15 minutes

250 g (8 oz) pasta (fusilli or similar)
3 tablespoons olive oil
2 whole garlic cloves, peeled
about 20 prawns, uncooked (or frozen)
about 20 cherry tomatoes
salt and freshly ground black pepper

Bring a pan of water to the boil. Add a pinch of salt and cook the pasta until just tender.

Meanwhile, heat the oil in a frying pan, add the whole garlic cloves and brown the prawns. Add the tomatoes and heat through. Remove the garlic cloves, then combine the prawns and tomatoes with the cooked and drained pasta.

Season to taste and serve.

Good tomato sauce

Serves 6
Preparation time: 15 minutes
Cooking time: 25 minutes

1 tablespoon olive oil
1 garlic clove, crushed
500 g (1 lb) ripe tomatoes, skinned, deseeded and chopped (or 700–800 g canned tomatoes)
1 tablespoon chopped parsley
1 tablespoon chopped basil
1 teaspoon sugar
1 teaspoon tomato purée
2 tablespoons red wine
salt and freshly ground black pepper

In a large pan, heat the oil and brown the crushed garlic for a few seconds, then add the tomatoes, herbs and sugar. Simmer for 10 minutes.

Add the tomato purée and wine and cook for a further 15 minutes.

Season to taste and serve with pasta or meat and a sprinkling of grated Parmesan or pecorino cheese.

Broccoli, pine nut and mascarpone pasta

Serves 6
Preparation time: 5 minutes
Cooking time: 15 minutes

375 g (12 oz) pasta (fusilli or similar)
200 g (7 oz) pine nuts
2 heads of broccoli
1 small tub of mascarpone cheese
salt and freshly ground black pepper

Cook the pasta in a pan of salted boiling water until just tender.

Meanwhile, toast the pine nuts in a dry frying pan and set aside. Steam or boil the broccoli, then cut into small florets.

Combine the broccoli with the pasta, then stir in half the pine nuts and the mascarpone. Season to taste. Top with the remaining pine nuts and serve immediately.

Red pesto pasta

Serves 4
Preparation time: 5 minutes
Cooking time: 15 minutes

250 g (8 oz) pasta (spaghetti or tagliatelle)
2 tablespoons pine nuts
2 tablespoons chopped Parmesan cheese
1 tablespoon sun-dried tomato purée
1–2 tablespoons olive oil
sea salt and freshly ground black pepper

Bring a pan of water to the boil, add a pinch of salt and cook the pasta until just tender.

Meanwhile, blend all the remaining ingredients to a smooth paste in a food processor or with a pestle and mortar, adding the oil a little at a time if the pesto sauce is too thick.

Drain the pasta, combine with the pesto sauce and serve.

Rice salad with optional olives

A great classic which, in my house at any rate, always goes down well with the olives served as an optional extra. This salad is always high in good nutritional things and low in saucepans, colanders, rinsing and the like if you make it with magical frozen cooked rice.

Serves 6
Preparation time: 10 minutes
Cooking time: 10 minutes

500g (1 lb) bag frozen cooked basmati rice
4 tomatoes
4 eggs
1 medium can sweetcorn
1 medium can tuna in its own juices/brine
olives (optional)
salt and freshly ground black pepper

For the vinaigrette dressing:
1 tablespoon wine vinegar
1 tablespoon Dijon mustard
4 tablespoons olive oil
sea salt and freshly ground black pepper

Place the rice in a mixing bowl and defrost in a microwave oven.

Place the tomatoes in a bowl and pour over boiling water to cover. Leave for 1–2 minutes, then drain, cut a cross at the stem end of each tomato, peel off the skins, and cut into small pieces.

Boil the eggs for 7–8 minutes, remove the shells and leave to cool slightly before cutting into pieces.

Open and drain the cans of sweetcorn and tuna, then combine all the ingredients with the rice. Season to taste.

To make the vinaigrette dressing, place all the ingredients in a jam jar, screw on the lid tightly and shake vigorously.

Serve separately with the rice salad – and olives (or not, as the case may be).

Four ideas brimful of good things – any leftovers can be eaten up for a picnic lunch the next day.

Cheddar coleslaw minus the onions

Serves 4
Preparation time: 5 minutes

2 tablespoons light mayonnaise
1 tablespoon single cream
salt and freshly ground black pepper
½ packet coleslaw mix (grated carrots and cabbage)
75 g (3 oz) Cheddar cheese, grated
2 tablespoons sultanas
1 orange, cut into small slices

Combine the mayonnaise, cream and a little salt and pepper to make a sauce. Pour over the remaining ingredients, stir thoroughly to mix, then serve.

Vegetable and smoked salmon frittata

Serves 4
Cooking time: 10 minutes

20 g (¾ oz) unsalted butter
4 tablespoons frozen sliced mixed vegetables
5 eggs
2 tablespoons single cream
freshly ground black pepper
2 slices good quality smoked salmon, organic if possible, cut into strips

Melt the butter in a frying pan and brown the vegetables. Lightly beat the eggs with the cream, add a little pepper, and pour over the vegetables.

When the eggs begin to set, top with the strips of smoked salmon and remove from the heat.

Haricot bean and peanut butter dip

Serves 4
Preparation time: 5 minutes

400 g (14 oz) can haricot beans, drained
2 tablespoons crunchy peanut butter
juice of 1 lemon

Purée the haricot beans in a liquidizer, then add the peanut butter, lemon juice and a little water if necessary.

Serve as a dip with crunchy vegetables and some tortilla chips.

Bulgar wheat, pineapple, hazelnut and smoked chicken salad

Serves 4
Preparation time: 10 minutes

8 tablespoons bulgar wheat, prepared according to the instructions on the packet
3 tablespoons pineapple chunks
2 tablespoons hazelnuts
300 g (10 oz) smoked chicken, cut into strips
olive oil
juice of ½ lemon
salt and freshly ground black pepper

Combine all the salad ingredients and dress with the oil, lemon juice and salt and pepper.

Escalopes of veal with apple

Serves 4
Preparation time: 5 minutes
Cooking time: approx. 10 minutes

50 g (2 oz) butter
4 veal escalopes
6 cooking apples, peeled and sliced
1 small pot crème fraîche
sea salt and freshly ground black pepper

In a large frying pan, heat the butter until it sizzles. Brown the escalopes for 1 minute on each side, then reduce the heat, add the apples and cook for 5–8 minutes, watching carefully.

Remove the meat and apples and set aside in a warm place. Add the cream to the frying pan and stir well, scraping off all the sticky deposits. When the sauce is very hot, season to taste, pour over the meat and serve immediately.

Loin of lamb, olive oil mashed potato and roasted vegetables with goat's cheese

Serves 4
Preparation time: 5 minutes
Cooking time: 20 minutes

6–8 floury potatoes, peeled and cut into pieces
150 ml (¼ pint) single cream
flavoursome olive oil
2 small loins of lamb
½ packet frozen roasted vegetables
1 fresh goat's cheese, crumbled
sea salt and freshly ground black pepper

Preheat the oven to 220°C (425°F), gas mark 7.

Boil the potatoes. When cooked, drain and mash together with the cream, a little oil, sea salt and pepper.

Meanwhile, place the loins of lamb in the oven and roast for 15–20 minutes.

Place the vegetables on a baking sheet and roast for 15–20 minutes.

Sprinkle the crumbled goat's cheese over the vegetables and serve with the mashed potato.

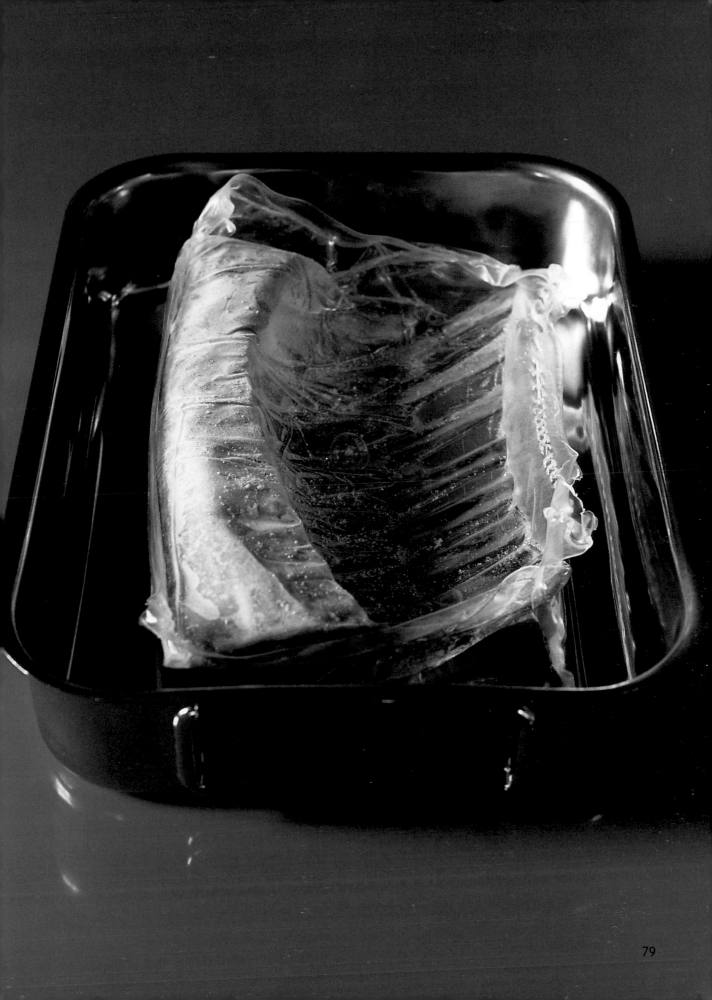

Blinis with beetroot, crème fraîche, salmon and dill

Serves 4
Preparation time: 5 minutes
Cooking time: 5 minutes

250 g (8 oz) fresh salmon, organic if possible
50 g (2 oz) cooked beetroot, finely diced
4 tablespoons crème fraîche
rind and juice of 1 lemon
1 tablespoon fresh dill (optional)
sea salt and freshly ground black pepper
4 blinis

Briefly steam or microwave the salmon, then flake it into small pieces and combine with the beetroot, crème fraîche, lemon rind and juice and dill.

Season to taste and serve with hot blinis.

Brie, apple and tomato toastie

Serves 4
Preparation time: 5 minutes
Cooking time: 5 minutes

4 slices white or wholemeal bread
2 tomatoes, finely sliced
200 g (7 oz) good quality, ripe, tasty Brie, cut into slices
1 Granny Smith apple, skin on, finely sliced

Assemble the ingredients one on top of the other on the bread and grill for 3–5 minutes.

Serve hot with tomato chutney.

Patatas bravas

Serves 4
Preparation time: 10 minutes
Cooking time: 15 minutes

2 tablespoons olive oil
175 g (6 oz) mild chorizo sausage, finely sliced
375 g (12 oz) potatoes, peeled and sliced
1 red onion, peeled and finely chopped
400 g (14 oz) can chopped tomatoes
pinch of Cayenne pepper (optional)

Heat the oil in a frying pan and fry the chorizo for a few minutes.

Add the potatoes and onion and continue to cook until soft and golden.

Add the tomatoes and Cayenne pepper, if using, then simmer for a further 15 minutes until the potatoes are cooked through and the liquid from the tomatoes has evaporated.

Sweet-and-sour stir-fried duck with vegetables

Serves 4
Cooking time: 4–8 minutes

1–2 tablespoons olive oil
2–3 duck breasts, sliced
1 packet of ready-prepared stir-fry vegetables, available pre-packed from the supermarket salad section
3–4 tablespoons Chinese sweet-and-sour sauce
sea salt and freshly ground black pepper

Heat the oil in the wok, then add the duck and vegetables.

When the meat and vegetables have begun to brown, add the sauce and stir well. Leave to caramelize for 1–2 minutes, then season to taste and serve immediately.

Chilli with sausages

Serves 4
Preparation time: 5 minutes
Cooking time: 10 minutes

2 tablespoons olive oil
2 red onions, peeled and finely chopped
6 sausages, sliced
400 g (14 oz) can tomatoes
1 red pepper, finely diced
1 tablespoon tomato purée
500 g (1 lb) can red kidney beans, drained and rinsed
salt and freshly ground black pepper
pinch of chilli powder
1 tablespoon crème fraîche
6 tacos

Heat the oil in a saucepan, add the onion and fry for a few minutes.

Add the sausage slices and brown. Add the tomatoes, red pepper, tomato purée and a little water. Bring to the boil and cook for 5 minutes before adding the red kidney beans. Simmer for a further 2–3 minutes, then season to taste with salt, pepper and chilli powder.

Serve with 1 tablespoon of crème fraîche and the tacos.

Herb sausages with lentils

Serves 4
Preparation time: 10 minutes
Cooking time: 10 minutes

2 tablespoons olive oil
1 red onion, peeled and chopped
50 g (2 oz) smoked bacon, cut into small pieces
150 g (5 oz) herb sausages, sliced
400 g (13 oz) can lentils, drained
2 tablespoons tomato purée
2 tomatoes, cut into quarters

Heat the olive oil in a frying pan. Add the onion, bacon pieces and sausage slices and cook for a few minutes, before adding the lentils, tomato purée and a little water.

Stir well to combine, then simmer for 5 minutes. Add the tomato quarters, heat through and serve.

Spicy sausage, prune and orange kebabs

Serves 4
Preparation time: 10 minutes
Cooking time: 15 minutes

4 spicy sausages (ideally French merguez sausages, if available), sliced
8 cherry tomatoes
1 red onion, cut into quarters
8 prunes, pitted
1 orange, cut into quarters
olive oil

Preheat the oven to 200°C (400°F), gas mark 6.

If using wooden kebab skewers, soak them in water first. Thread the ingredients alternately onto the skewers, brush with oil, place in an ovenproof dish and roast in the oven for about 15 minutes, turning occasionally.

Serve with raisin couscous.

Tomato and sausage risotto

Serves 4
Preparation time: 5 minutes
Cooking time: 25 minutes

3 tablespoons olive oil
1 red onion, peeled and chopped
250 g (8 oz) arborio rice
400 g (14 oz) can chopped tomatoes
500 ml (17 fl oz) vegetable stock, made from a stock cube
4 sausages
50 g (2 oz) freshly grated Parmesan cheese

Heat the oil in a frying pan and fry the onion. Add the rice and cook for 2 minutes until the grains become translucent. Add the chopped tomatoes and a little stock, stir well, bring to the boil, then simmer until the liquid has been absorbed. Gradually add the remaining stock, a ladleful at a time, stirring and simmering until each addition is absorbed. This should take about 15 minutes, after which the rice should be deliciously creamy.

Meanwhile, fry the sausages in another frying pan.

Combine the sausages with the rice, season to taste, sprinkle with the Parmesan, and serve.

Chilli hot dogs

Serves 4
Preparation time: 5 minutes
Cooking time: 5 minutes

4 frankfurter sausages
2 baguettes or French sticks
4 tablespoons Chilli con carne (see page 20)
tomato ketchup, to serve

Cook the sausages in boiling water for 5 minutes. Split open the bread slices, insert the sausages and top with a spoonful of Chilli con carne (see page 20) and a dollop of tomato ketchup.

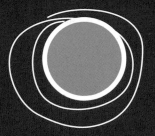

From time to time

When there's something to celebrate, we drop all (or nearly all) our principles about eating healthily and cook solely for pleasure.

For birthdays and Hallow'Een, sugar is the order of the day. Children tuck into sweets, chocolate and fizzy drinks. And as it's the exception, rather than the rule, it doesn't really matter.

From time to time, they will want to do everything themselves, like the grown-ups, whether it's to please us, or to make cakes and cookies for school. It's important to come up with easy things that don't involve too many complicated or technical baking stages, so that success is guaranteed, which will encourage them to do even better next time.

Tea party treats for the girls

Big starters for little people

Makes 6–8 canapés
Preparation time: 15 minutes

1 small pot taramasalata
4 large slices white bread
2 slices ham
radishes and baby onion slices

Spread the taramasalata on 2 slices of bread and
place the ham on the remaining 2 slices. Using
a sharp (careful!) pastry-cutter, cut out circles.
Decorate with the radish and onion slices and
serve as canapés 'like the grown-ups'.

90

Ice cream floats

Serves 6
Preparation time: 3 minutes

1 bottle lemonade
6 tablespoons grenadine (or blackcurrant) cordial
6 scoops vanilla ice cream

Place 1 tablespoon of grenadine cordial in each glass. Pour in lemonade, leaving sufficient room to then carefully place a ball of ice cream in each glass. Wait until it produces froth, then serve immediately with spoons and straws.

Tagada strawberry mousse

Serves 6
Preparation time: 5 minutes
Chilling time: 2 hours

250 ml (8 fl oz) whipping cream
About 15 Haribo Tagada foamy strawberries,
plus extra for decoration.

Pour the cream into a saucepan and heat with
the sweets. Stir until the sweets have completely
dissolved, taking care that the mixture does not
boil. Pour the mixture into a bowl and leave to
cool completely in a refrigerator.

Using an electric mixer, beat the cream mixture
into a mouse.

Serve in small glasses and top with foamy
strawberries.

Acid cake

This cake will have no trouble satisfying the ultra-acid tastes of chip fans and other desperados.

Serves 10
Preparation time: 15 minutes
Cooking time: 25 minutes

For the sponge cake:
225 g (7½ oz) soft margarine or very soft unsalted butter
225 g (7½ oz) plain flour
220 g (7¼ oz) sugar
4 eggs
2 level teaspoons baking powder
rind of 1 lemon
(or, if absolutely desperate, a packet of cake mix)

For the icing:
400 g (13–14 oz) icing sugar
180 g (6 oz) unsalted butter
3 tablespoons lemon curd, or the juice and rind of
2 lemons

To decorate:
1 packet 'Flying Saucers' or similar sherbet sweets

Preheat the oven to 180°C (350°F), gas mark 4.

Grease and flour a deep cake tin.

Place all the ingredients in the mixing bowl and, using an electric mixer, beat for 2 minutes until the mixture is smooth.

Turn the mixture into the prepared cake tin and bake for about 25 minutes, checking 5 minutes before the end.

Remove the cake from the oven and leave to cool in the tin before turning out.

To make the butter icing, place all the ingredients in the mixing bowl and, using an electric mixer, beat until smooth and creamy.

Cut the cooled cake into 2 layers and sandwich together with the icing, spreading it with a spatula. (It's a good idea to spread a little icing onto the surface of the top layer first so that the Flying Saucers can get a grip!) Press the sweets onto the top of the cake and tie a ribbon around the sides.

Fairy cakes

These mini-sponge cakes are a favourite children's tea party treat. To the mind of the creative confectioner, they are like a blank canvas. Make dozens and dozens of them, then enjoy decorating them with your children. (To save you the trouble of hunting round in vain, turn to the back of the book for the suppliers' addresses for the decorations in the photograph.)

Makes 12
Preparation time: 3 minutes
Cooking time: 20 minutes

150 g (5 oz) soft margarine or very soft unsalted butter
5 oz caster sugar
175 g (6 oz) plain flour
1½ teaspoons baking powder
3 eggs

Preheat the oven to 180°C (350°F), gas mark 4.

Place all the ingredients in a large mixing bowl and, using an electric mixer, beat for 1–2 minutes until the mixture is smooth.

Place 12 paper cake cases in a bun tin and divide the mixture between them.

Bake for about 20 minutes. The cakes should be lightly golden and firm.

Transfer the cakes to a wire rack and leave to cool completely.

Glacé icing

4 tablespoons lemon juice
200 g (7 oz) icing sugar

I prefer to cover the top of the cakes completely with icing to make a flat and smooth surface for the decorations.

Combine sufficient lemon juice with the sugar to make a spreading icing and cover each cake. Leave to set.

Frozen strawberry and mascarpone cheesecake

Serves 8–10
Preparation time: 10 minutes
Chilling time: 2 hours

250 g (8 oz) mascarpone cheese
500 g (1 lb) good quality cream cheese
150 g (5 oz) icing sugar
250 g (8 oz) ripe and tasty strawberries
sugar mice (to decorate)

Hull the strawberries and purée in a food processor or blender.

Beat together the mascarpone, cream cheese and sugar. Add the strawberry purée, stir well and pour into a flexible silicon or ordinary loaf tin lined with clingfilm, leaving some hanging over the edges to make handles to help unmould the cake.

Chill in a refrigerator for 2–3 hours.

Turn the cake out of the tin and decorate 15 minutes before serving.

You-know-who's iced chocolate cake

Seeing as it's you, I'll give you another chance to try two recipes, one of which has become an outright classic. They are SO easy, SO good and SO impressive that once again I'm giving them a place of their own. After all, perhaps you haven't already got my other books!

Serves 6–8
Preparation time: 5 minutes
Cooking time: 22 minutes

200 g (7 oz) good quality dark chocolate
200 g (7 oz) unsalted butter
220 g (7½ oz) sugar
5 eggs
1 tablespoon plain flour

Preheat the oven to 190°C (375°F), gas mark 5. Grease and flour a deep cake tin.

Melt the chocolate with the butter in a microwave oven, bain-marie, or bowl over a pan of hot water. (Do not let the bowl touch the water.) Stir in the sugar and leave to cool slightly. Incorporate the eggs one by one, beating well with a wooden spoon after each addition. Finally, add the flour and stir until the mixture is smooth.

Turn the mixture into the cake tin and bake for 22 minutes. The cake should not be fully set in the middle.

Remove the cake from the oven, leave to cool for just a few minutes before turning out and leaving to cool completely. It tastes even better if left overnight!

Easy-peasy icing

4 tablespoons water
200 g (7 oz) dark chocolate
100 g (3½ oz) unsalted butter

Heat all the ingredients together in a microwave oven, bain-marie, or bowl over a pan of hot water. (Do not let the bowl touch the water.)

Stir well until the icing is perfectly smooth. Place the cake on a wire rack over a sheet of greaseproof paper or acetate. Leave the icing mixture to cool slightly so that it is not too liquid, then spread over the cake.

Barbie cake

Serves 10–12
Preparation time: 15 minutes
Cooking time: 50 minutes

150 g (5 oz) yogurt
150 ml (¼ pint) milk
250 g (8 oz) soft margarine or very soft butter
375 g (12 oz) sugar
7 eggs
500 g (1 lb) plain flour
3 teaspoons baking powder

Preheat the oven to 190°C (375°F), gas mark 5.

Grease and flour a 2 litre (3½ pint) pudding basin.

Combine the yogurt with the milk and set aside.

Cream the butter and sugar together until light and fluffy. Add the eggs one by one, beating after each addition.

Gradually stir in the flour and the yogurt-milk mixture alternately, beating well at each stage. Add the baking powder and beat again.

Turn the mixture into the prepared pudding basin and bake for about 50 minutes, reducing the heat to 180°C (350°F), gas mark 4 after 30–40 minutes.

Remove the cake from the oven, turn it out onto a wire rack and leave to cool completely before setting to work.

At the back of the book you will find a list of addresses where you can buy the full range of 'half-Barbie' dolls on a stick to insert into the cake, as well as ready-made icing in all colours and sugar decorations. (If you want to avoid all that, just use butter cream or chocolate icing. You could even mutilate a real Barbie doll and make it all yourself.)

Finally, all it takes to stick the icing to Barbie's plastic skin is a little apricot jam diluted slightly with water, a brush and a dash of dexterity (but not too much, I am terribly clumsy and I don't think mine turned out badly at all). Use some ribbon to cover any dubious areas. My sister-in-law, Margo, doesn't bother with a full skirt, which requires a large expanse of icing. She just makes lots of overhanging pieces and flounces.

Use your girls' storybooks for inspiration.

Cheats' marshmallow cake for the girls and candy-floss cake for the boys

A little bit of initiative is called for here to track down candy-floss in bags or tubs (try petrol station shops) and mini-marshmallows. Ready-made icing is easily come by now and can be found in the home-baking section of most supermarkets.

But I promise you, that is the only effort involved and is a small price to pay to amaze your children's guests (and, more importantly, their parents) when it comes to lighting the candles. You will see that the cake recipe is the same as for the simple 'Victoria sandwich', that great British classic that goes down well with all children. Trust me!

Serves 10
Preparation time: 5 minutes
Cooking time: 25 minutes

For the cake:
225 g (7½ oz) plain flour
225 g (7½ oz) soft margarine or very soft butter
220 g (7¼ oz) sugar
4 eggs
2 level teaspoons baking powder
1 teaspoon natural vanilla extract
(or a packet of plain cake mix for real cheats)

For the buttercream:
400 g (14 oz) icing sugar
175 g (6 oz) butter
juice of 1 lemon
(or simply 3–4 tablespoons raspberry jam)

about 300 g (10 oz) white fondant icing
1 packet mini marshmallows (for the girls)
1 bag candyfloss (for the boys)

Preheat the oven to 180°C (350°F), gas mark 4.

Grease and flour a deep cake tin.

Place all the ingredients in a mixing bowl and, using an electric mixer, beat for 2 minutes until the mixture is smooth.

Turn the mixture into the cake tin and bake for about 25 minutes, checking after 20 minutes to see if it is cooked.

Remove the cake from the oven and leave to cool before turning out.

Place all the buttercream ingredients in a mixing bowl and, using an electric mixer, beat until the mixture is smooth and creamy.

Cut the cake into two layers and sandwich together with the jam or the buttercream. If using buttercream, also cover the top and sides of the cake.

Dust a work surface with icing sugar and roll the fondant icing out into a circle large enough to cover the cake and fall down in pretty folds over the sides. Decorate with marshmallows for the girls and candy-floss for the boys, adding the candy-floss just before serving so that it does not collapse and turn soggy.

Last-minute tea party treats

If you have neither the time nor the motivation to have everything totally homemade, like ALL the other parties in the class; if you left it far too late to book an entertainer or magician… then just say to yourself that next year you'll churn the butter yourself for the sandwiches, that you'll grow your own strawberries in your kitchen garden and that you'll take evening classes in calligraphy and porcelain painting so that you can decorate the glasses and plates with the name of each little guest.

Then take particular care with the cake for the birthday child and take them on a tour of the supermarket, allowing them to choose anything they like, even things that rarely make an appearance inside your cupboards and fridge, which, at all other times of the year, are of course beyond reproach in terms of healthy eating.

Alphabet cake

Serves 10 (or 26)
Preparation time: 25 minutes
Cooking time: 25 minutes
Chilling time: 1 hour for the decoration

For the letters:
200 g (7 oz) dark chocolate, melted
{don't panic, details of where you can get the mould are given at the back of the book. (If that's no good, you can buy them ready-made from other addresses also listed at the back of the book.)

For the cake:
225 g (7½ oz) soft margarine or very soft butter
225 g (7½ oz) plain flour
225 g (7½ oz) sugar
4 eggs
4 tablespoons cocoa powder combined with
4 tablespoons hot water
2 level teaspoons baking powder

For the icing:
500 g (1 lb) icing sugar
200 g (7 oz) butter, softened
2 tablespoons water
250 g (8 oz) good quality milk chocolate (preferably couverture chocolate)

Start with the letters...

Melt the chocolate in a microwave oven, bain-marie, or bowl over a pan of hot water.

If you have managed to track down some couverture chocolate, microwaving will present no problems. Nestlé's milk chocolate also works very well. If your chocolate is not top quality, it is best to melt it in a bain-marie, or bowl over a pan of hot water (not allowing the bowl to touch the water).

Place a sheet of greaseproof paper or acetate over your work surface.

Pour the chocolate into the letter mould. Using a spatula, preferably an angled one, ensure that all the letters are properly filled with melted chocolate. Tap the sides of the mould to release any air bubbles to the surface.

Scrape the surface of the mould, letting any excess chocolate run down onto the paper or acetate. Place the mould in the refrigerator for 1 hour.

Then make the cake...

Preheat the oven to 180°C (350°F), gas mark 4.

Grease and flour a deep cake tin – try to find a superb square one like mine, which is great for arranging the letters in straight lines. (Please note that for the large cake in the photograph, I doubled the quantities. And I can let you into a little secret: it also works very well with bought cake mixes.)

Place all the ingredients in a food processor (I love this recipe!) and beat for 2 minutes until the mixture is smooth.

Turn the mixture into the prepared cake tin and bake for about 25 minutes – times vary with every oven. Watch carefully.

When the cake is cooked, leave it to cool slightly in the tin before turning it out onto a wire rack and leaving it to cool completely.

Meanwhile, make the icing...

Place all the ingredients in the food processor (having cleaned it out thoroughly first) and beat until the icing is smooth and creamy.

Cut the cold cake into two layers and sandwich together with the icing. Then cover the whole cake with icing using a smooth knife or a spatula.

Halve the quantities if you are not cutting the cake into two layers. Personally, I like to give it an air of importance by adding an extra layer of icing to make it just that little bit taller.

Twist the chocolate letter mould as you would an ice cube tray and turn the letters out onto a cloth so that they do not break.

Arrange the letters on the cake before cutting it all up and serving to the guests – if possible giving each one their own initial.

Big cake with little petits fours

If you haven't got an alphabet mould, decorating the cake with tiny petits fours will give just as much, if not more pleasure.

Piñata

A party game from South America that will get even the most placid guest going! (See page 192.)

Serve crisps with the peanut butter dip, chilli hot dogs and grilled fresh pineapple before producing the birthday child's cake.

Hallow'Een

A morbid imagination is the main ingredient of these two little recipes.

Gut soup

Serves 4
Cooking time: 15 minutes

250 g (8 oz) pasta in a variety of shapes
(such as tagliatelle, fusilli, penne)
each requiring the same cooking time if possible
750 ml (1¼ pints) tomato juice, fresh if possible
2–3 tablespoons Worcestershire sauce
salt and freshly ground black pepper

Cook the pasta. Heat the tomato juice and combine with the 'guts'.

Season with the Worcestershire sauce, salt and pepper.

Mud and worms

Serves 4
Preparation time: 5 minutes

1 packet chocolate shortbread biscuits,
or chocolate digestives
2 tablespoons blanched hazelnuts
2 tablespoons raisins
150 ml (¼ pint) single cream
200 g (7 oz) milk chocolate
liquorice bootlaces for the worms

In a large mixing bowl, crush the biscuits by hand. Add the hazelnuts and raisins.

Bring the cream just to the boil and pour over the chocolate.

Stir until the chocolate has melted, then combine with the crushed biscuits.

Serve with the liquorice worms.

Thank goodness for toffee apples – an infinitely less gory Hallow'Een treat!

Irish apple pie

Far be it from me to impose any nationalist attachment to the past on my children, but they really do prefer Hallow'Een (yes, that is the correct spelling) County-Antrim style. Before the advent of orange plastic sheeting, it was a family party with disguises rarely going beyond black cats, witches, vampires and ghosts. The apple was the central ingredient, both in games and in dishes. We would hide lucky coins in apple pies in much the same way as we do with Christmas pudding.

Serves 6–8
Preparation time: 20 minutes
Resting time: 1 hour
Cooking time: 30 minutes

350 g (11½ oz) plain flour
150 g (5 oz) butter, very cold and cut into small pieces
2 tablespoons sugar
1 egg, lightly beaten
750 g (1½ lb) cooking apples
75 g (3 oz) sugar
2 or 3 small coins wrapped in kitchen foil
a little milk to glaze

Place the flour in a large mixing bowl, and rub in the butter until the mixture resembles fine breadcrumbs. Add the 2 tablespoons of sugar, the egg and enough cold water to form a soft dough. Wrap in clingfilm and leave in the refrigerator for 1–2 hours.

Preheat the oven to 200°C (400°F), gas mark 6.

Knead the pastry for a few minutes on a cold and lightly floured work surface. Roll out ⅔ of the dough and use to line the base of a 28-cm (11-inch) tart tin.

Peel and slice the apples. Arrange over the pastry base, sprinkle with the sugar and tuck in the coins.

Roll out the remaining pastry, place over the apples, pressing down firmly at the edges to seal, first with the fingertips, then with a fork. Brush the top with a little milk to glaze. Make a slit in the centre, or prick with a fork, and bake for 30 minutes until golden.

Serve the pie hot with mascarpone, vanilla ice cream or custard.

Duck apple

Float some apples in a large bowl of water. The people playing the game have to try to munch their way through them while keeping their hands behind their backs.

Hallow'Een
Bob apple

Pass a fairly thick piece of string through the apples and suspend them from the ceiling. The players have to try to be the first to sink their teeth into and then eat the apples, without using their arms or hands.

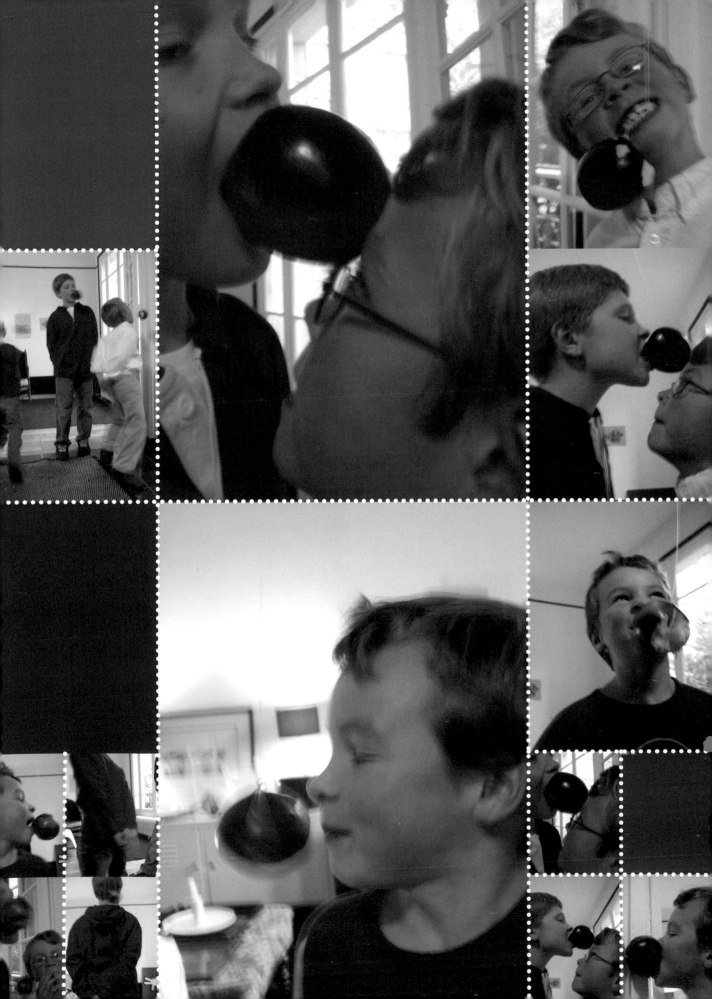

Summer camp

There's no need to go far. A simple tent in the garden and a little imagination will transform your children into real adventurers. It's best to pitch camp near the house in case of night-time fears or rain.

These recipes are extremely simple, although adults and antiseptic cream will need to be close at hand. They require a minimum of equipment, cutlery and crockery.

Grilled mackerel with lime

Serves 6
Preparation time: 5 minutes
Cooking time: 5–8 minutes

6 mackerel, gutted
3 limes, very finely sliced
olive oil
sea salt and freshly ground black pepper

Make slits in the sides of the fish and insert the lime slices.

Brush the fish with a little olive oil, season with salt and pepper and grill over the camp fire.

Mini-mixed sausage and pineapple kebabs

Serves 6
Preparation time: 5 minutes
Cooking time: 5 minutes

About 30 small, tasty butcher's sausages
1 can pineapple chunks, drained

If using wooden skewers, soak them first in water.
Thread the sausages and pineapple chunks
alternately onto the skewers, then grill over the fire.

From time to time

Toasted marshmallows

This must be THE camp fire recipe of all time, certainly ever since the Stone Age.

It's always a delight to crunch through the thin layer of caramel that appears as if by magic after only a few seconds in the flames.

Blackened bananas with lemon butter

Serves 6
Preparation time: 10 minutes
Cooking time: 15 minutes

juice and grated rind of ½ lemon
1 tablespoon sugar
100 g (3 ½ oz) butter
6 small bananas

Combine the lemon juice and rind with the sugar and butter, then leave in a cool place.

Place the bananas, skins on, on a sheet of kitchen foil on the barbecue grill and leave them to blacken for about 15 minutes. Split the bananas open and insert a little lemon butter before tucking in.

Toasted Snickers sandwiches

Serves 6
Preparation time: 5 minutes
Cooking time: 5 minutes

50 g (2 oz) butter
12 small slices white bread
3 Snickers bars, sliced

Butter the slices of bread. Place one of the slices, buttered side down, in an old griddle pan. Top with a few slices of Snickers bar and cover with a second slice of bread, buttered side up. Place the griddle pan over the fire and toast for a few minutes.

Real hot chocolate

Serves 6
Preparation time: 3 minutes

1 litre (1¾ pints) full-fat milk
500 ml (17 fl oz) single cream
400 g (13 oz) good quality cooking chocolate,
chopped or grated
whipped cream
hundreds and thousands
marshmallows
chocolate powder

Combine the milk with the cream and bring to
the boil.

Pour over the chocolate and stir until it has melted.

Pour the chocolate mixture into the cups and
decorate with whipped cream, hundreds and
thousands, marshmallows, chocolate powder and
any more of your children's favourite toppings.

School

Lunchbox

Whether it's instead of school dinners or for the summer term trip, we all know the phenomenon of the remains of packed lunches reduced to crumbs in the bottom of the rucksack. The only things that have actually been eaten are the cake intended for teatime and the sweets kindly brought by a friend.

Stick to your guns. Try not to give in each time to requests for bags of crisps, cans of fizzy drinks and packets of ultra-sweet biscuits and cakes on the pretext that 'at least they'll eat something'.

Here are a few ideas for more balanced packed lunches that they might even enjoy.

1 Vary the bread. Try to avoid sliced white bread or French bread. Wholemeal bread or muffins provide more fibre. You can also vary the flavours by using Italian bread, tortilla wraps, naan and pita breads, which are also available in 'mini' versions.

2 Always provide a vegetable. Cherry tomatoes, baby cucumbers and steamed baby sweetcorn are all easy to nibble. Combine grated carrots with tuna, hummus or chicken, and always slip a lettuce leaf in the ham sandwich.

3 Grapes, baby bananas, plums and clementines always go down well with children. With their thicker skins, they are easier to peel and to eat than strawberries, peaches or pears. Try adding oranges, pineapple, apples and pears to individual salad portions based on pasta, couscous, potatoes or green beans, with or without meat.

4 Dried fruits, such as apricots, pears and prunes, are now available in softer, ready-to-eat versions, sometimes flavoured with orange or vanilla and sold in little bags. A great source of energy and vitamins for powerful playtimes.

5 As for dairy products, your task is easy. They now come in all sorts of forms: in bags, little pots, devices to suck or on sticks.

Bramble and apple muffins

Makes about 12
Preparation time: 10 minutes
Cooking time: 20–25 minutes

2 eggs
125 ml (4 fl oz) vegetable oil
200 g (7 oz) sugar
250 ml (8 fl oz) milk
375 g (12 oz) plain flour
4 teaspoons baking powder
3 apples, peeled and finely diced
200 g (7 oz) blackberries

Preheat the oven to 200°C (400°F), gas mark 6.

Place the eggs, oil, sugar and milk in a large mixing bowl and beat well. Sift in the flour and baking powder, then beat again. Carefully fold in the apple pieces and blackberries.

Place the muffin cases in the muffin tin and fill each case 2/3 full. Place in the preheated oven and bake for 20–25 minutes.

Banana and chocolate chip muffins

Makes about 12
Preparation time: 5 minutes
Cooking time: 20–25 minutes

1 egg
400 ml (14 fl oz) vegetable oil
3 ripe bananas, crushed
400 ml (14 fl oz) milk
250 g (8 oz) plain flour
100 g (3½ oz) chocolate chips
125 g (4 oz) sugar
6 teaspoons baking powder

Preheat the oven to 200°C (400°F), gas mark 6.

In a large mixing bowl, beat together the egg, oil, bananas and milk. Sift in the flour and add the chocolate chips, sugar and baking powder and beat again.

Place the muffin cases in the muffin tin and fill each case 2/3 full.

Bake in the preheated oven for 20–25 minutes.

Mini raspberry muffins

Makes about 36
Preparation time: 10 minutes
Cooking time: 20–25 minutes

250 g (8 oz) plain flour
85 g (3 oz) sugar
2 level teaspoons baking powder
1 large egg
200 ml (7 fl oz) milk
90 g (3¼ oz) butter, melted
120 g (4 oz) fresh raspberries

Preheat the oven to 200°C (400°F), gas mark 6.

Sift the flour and baking powder together in a large mixing bowl and add the sugar. Make a well in the centre.

In another bowl, beat together the egg, milk and melted butter, then pour this mixture into the well and stir until the mixture is as smooth as possible, but don't worry if there are still a few lumps.

Gently fold in the raspberries, taking care not to break them up too much.

Place mini-muffin cases in a muffin tin and fill 2/3 full with the mixture.

Bake for about 20–25 minutes in the preheated oven until the muffins have risen well and are beautifully golden.

Madeira cake

Serves 6–8
Preparation time: 10 minutes
Cooking time: 50 minutes

4 eggs
weight of the eggs in butter plus a little extra
for greasing the baking tin
weight of the eggs in caster sugar
weight of the eggs in plain flour, sifted
1½ teaspoons baking powder

Preheat the oven to 180°C (350°F), gas mark 4.

Grease a deep 20 cm (8 inch) cake tin, unless you
are using a silicon one.

Cream together the butter and sugar until the
mixture is very smooth. Add the eggs, beating
constantly, then add the flour and baking powder.

Turn the mixture into the prepared tin and bake for
40–50 minutes. Leave to cool slightly before turning
out onto a wire rack and leaving to cool completely.

Blondies

Makes about 20 squares
Preparation time: 10 minutes
Cooking time: 20 minutes

300 g (10 oz) white chocolate, made with cocoa butter
75 g (3 oz) unsalted butter
3 eggs
80 g (3 oz) soft brown sugar
210 g (7 oz) plain flour
100 g (3½ oz) soft, ready-to-eat dried apricots, finely diced
1 tablespoon lemon juice

Preheat the oven to 190°C (375°F), gas mark 5.

Grease and flour a rectangular baking tin measuring
roughly 28 x 23 cm (11 x 8 inches).

Place the chocolate and butter in a bowl and melt
gently in a microwave oven, bain-marie or bowl over
a pan of hot water. Add the eggs and sugar, beating
constantly, followed by the remaining ingredients.

Turn the mixture into the prepared baking tin, spread
out evenly, and bake for about 20 minutes until the
top is lightly golden.

Leave to cool completely in the baking tin, then cut
into small squares.

Carrot cake

Preparation time: 20 minutes
Cooking time: 50 minutes

5 eggs, separated
200 g (7 oz) sugar
rind of 1 orange, grated
200 g (7 oz) ground almonds
250 g (8 oz) carrots, peeled and grated
200 g (7 oz) icing sugar
juice of 1 lemon

Grease a deep, 25 cm (10 inch) baking tin.

Preheat the oven to 160°C (325°F), gas mark 3.

Beat the egg yolks with the sugar until the mixture is
pale and creamy. Add the orange rind and ground
almonds, and stir well.

Whisk the egg whites into stiff peaks, then gently
fold into the almond-egg yolk mixture, together with
the grated carrots.

Turn the mixture into the prepared baking tin and
bake in the centre of the oven for about 50 minutes.
The cake should spring back when you press the
centre with your finger. If the cake shows signs of
browning too quickly, cover with kitchen foil.

Remove the cake from the oven and leave to cool
for 5 minutes before turning out onto a wire rack.

To make the icing, combine the icing sugar with the
lemon juice and spread over the cake when it is
completely cold.

Breakfast labour of love

It must be a sentimental rite of passage, because children often want to make their parents breakfast in bed to mark occasions such as their birthdays, fathers' day or mothers' day. We gladly forget the lie-ins ruined by cold coffee and crumbs being scattered in the bed.

These recipes require just a simple heart-shaped pastry cutter and the minimum amount of technical skill.

Egg in toast

Serves 2
Preparation time: 5 minutes
Cooking time: 3 minutes

2 slices wholemeal bread
a little butter
2 eggs

Using the pastry cutter, cut out the heart shape from each slice of bread.

Heat the butter in a frying pan and fry the bread on one side.

Turn the bread over and break an egg into the heart-shaped hole. Cook for about 3 minutes.

Meanwhile, toast and butter the heart-shaped pieces of bread. Serve hot.

Toasted brioche hearts with chocolate and muscovado butter

Serves 2
Preparation time: 5 minutes
Cooking time: 2 minutes

1 teaspoon cocoa powder
1 teaspoon muscovado or soft brown sugar
50 g (2 oz) butter
2 slices brioche

Combine the cocoa powder, sugar and butter.

Using a heart-shaped pastry cutter, cut out heart shapes from the brioche, then toast them.

Serve the brioche very hot with the chocolate butter in a separate dish.

Homemade lemonade

6 large, unwaxed lemons, finely sliced
250 g (8 oz) sugar
200 ml (7 fl oz) lemon juice, freshly squeezed
300 ml (½ pint) water
ice cubes
small bunch fresh mint (optional but delicious)

Set aside 1 or 2 lemon slices for decoration, then purée the remaining slices in a blender, together with 200 g (7 oz) sugar and the lemon juice. Pass this mixture through a fine sieve, pressing down firmly to extract all the juice. Add the water and the remaining sugar.

Place some ice cubes in a large jug, pour in the lemonade and leave to rest for 10 minutes.

Serve decorated with the reserved lemon slices and a few mint leaves.

Children in charge

Budget shopping

... and sweets!

What shall we do? Beef in red wine? Paella? Curry?

It's just as well I'm here!

Everything we need for a homemade fizzy drink.

I like that idea.

Let's start with the most important things: popcorn ...

At last they're getting themselves some carbohydrates!

Adèle takes things in hand. Some crème fraîche ...

... and some organic eggs like we have at home.

We're real cooks! All that without going over our budget!

Homemade pizzas

1 On a ready-made pizza base, spread a good tomato sauce (see page 72).

2 Everyone chooses their own toppings

5 Coco, in the middle, arranges the tomatoes.

6 Then a little mozzarella.

9 And there you have it! Bake in a preheated oven at 200°C (400°F), gas mark 6 for 10 minutes.

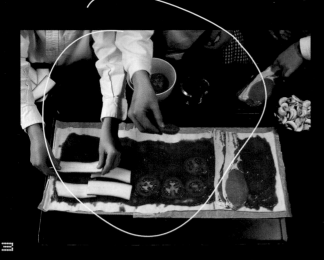

3

Tanguy, on the left, starts with thin slices of courgette.

4

Nicolas, on the right, prefers bacon.

7

Some finely sliced mushrooms, please ...

8

... some chorizo sausage and some olives

Pauline and Victoire's cookies

1 Can you see my biceps, Victoire?

2 Yes, but you've got to roll in both directions, Pauline.

3 They start at the edges.

4 I've not got much space left.

5 1, 2, 3, we press down together.

6 A change of technique.

It's the perfect culinary activity for young children who have great experience of modelling clay techniques. If you really must keep your kitchen clean and don't want to go through the theory of mixing, weighing and the like, then you will be glad to know that the mixture in the photos is ready-made. It is delicious and is intended for making Christmas tree decorations and other types of gingerbread men. (See what you can find in your supermarket's chilled baking-goods cabinet.) However, if you prefer, here is a recipe.

Makes about 30 cookies
Preparation time: 10 minutes
Cooking time: 15 minutes

50 g (2 oz) butter, very soft
100 g (3½ oz) brown sugar
1 tablespoon milk
160 g (5½ oz) plain flour

Preheat the oven to 180°C (350°F), gas mark 4.

Using an electric mixer, cream together the butter and sugar. Add the milk and beat until the mixture is very smooth.

Incorporate the flour and beat to form a soft dough.

Let the children roll out the pastry with a rolling pin and cut out shapes using a variety of pastry cutters.

Place the biscuits on an ovenproof baking sheet (either non-stick or placed on a sheet of greaseproof paper) and bake for 10–15 minutes until golden.

4 And they're off!

5 Not too near the middle, Pauline!

6 Look at yourself, Victoire!

10 Perhaps you were right after all!

12

11

Do you think Mum and Dad will appreciate everything we're doing for them? Quick! In the oven they go!

Philippine's apple tart

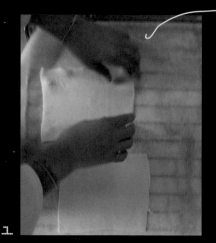

1\.

2\.

3\.

Ready-rolled puff pastry is a wonderful thing!
Leave enough space between the sheets of pastry.

I'm very careful when
I'm cutting the apples

4\.

A little sugar.

3–4 apples, peeled and finely sliced
1 packet frozen ready-rolled puff pastry
100 g (3½ oz) sugar

Arrange the apple slices on the pastry sheets leaving no gaps between the slices.

Sprinkle with the sugar and bake for 20–25 minutes – the tart should be beautifully golden on top.

Remove from the oven, serve with vanilla ice cream, for example, and enjoy!

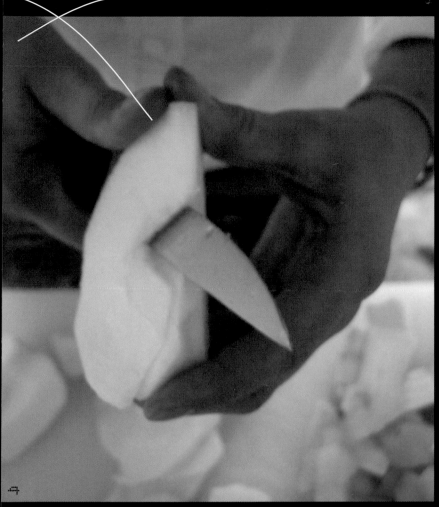

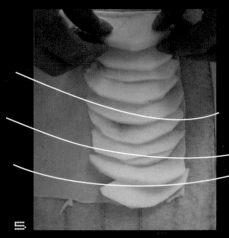

Years of practice!

And not the least bit frightened!

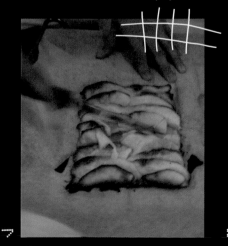

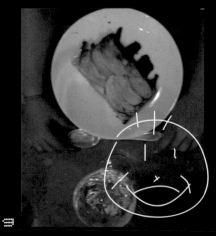

My tart is browned to perfection.

I'd like some more.

Wish granted!

Maxence's courgette flan

1. I wash the vegetables thoroughly

2. We don't want a slice of finger in it.

3. Summary of the ingredients

5. Isn't that pretty?

A little basil.

It goes down very well with my audience!

Paper means less washing up.

I'm concentrating.

Don't talk with your mouth full!

The personal touch!

You will need:
1 packet ready-rolled frozen shortcrust pastry, defrosted
a little low-fat soft cheese
2 tomatoes, not too juicy, sliced
3 courgettes, sliced
1 goat's cheese log, sliced
fresh herbs (such as basil and chives)
olive oil, salt and freshly ground black pepper

Preheat the oven to 150°C (300°F), gas mark 2.

Use a pastry sheet to line a flan dish and prick the base with a fork.

Spread the cream cheese over the base and arrange the sliced tomato, courgettes and cheese over the top.

Season with salt and pepper and drizzle with olive oil.

Bake in the centre of the oven for 45 minutes.

When ready to serve, garnish with snipped fresh herbs.

Arthur's tiramisu

You will need:
3 eggs
150 g (5 oz) caster sugar
250 g (8 oz) mascarpone cheese
1 tablespoon Amaretto or Marsala
2 packets sponge fingers (Boudoir biscuits)
500 ml (17 fl oz) cold instant coffee
cocoa powder or Nesquick

1

Take the eggs and separate the yolks from the whites.

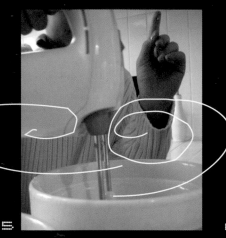

5

6

7

Beat the caster sugar with the egg yolks until the mixture is pale and fluffy.

Add the mascarpone and Amaretto and beat well.

11

12

13

Briefly dip the sponge fingers in the instant coffee.

Line the base of a large dish with sponge fingers, add a layer of the mascarpone mixture, another layer of sponge fingers, then finish with a layer of the mascarpone mixture.

Put the yolks in a large bowl and the whites in a medium-sized one.

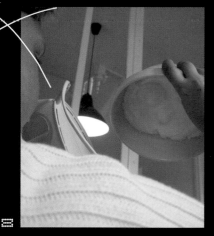

Add a pinch of salt to the egg whites and whisk into stiff peaks. (Check the egg whites are ready by turning the bowl upside down.)

Gently fold the egg whites into the mixture

Place in a refrigerator for at least 2 hours.

Just before serving, dust with cocoa powder using a tea strainer.

Elliott's quesadillos

Serves 2

some mozzarella cheese, sliced
2 tomatoes, sliced
4 tortilla wraps

Preheat the oven to 190°C (375°F), gas mark 5.

Place the mozzarella and tomato slices on one half of each of the tortilla wraps, then fold over the other half.

Bake for about 15 minutes and they're ready!

Enjoy!

1

Watch out for your fingers!

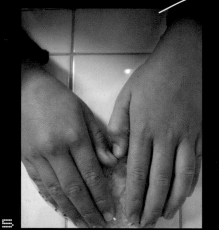

5

Press down firmly.

10

I have to do everything in this house!

5

Fold the top half down.

Then slice the mozzarella.

I've got my hands full.

Arrange the filling.

One for you and one for me.

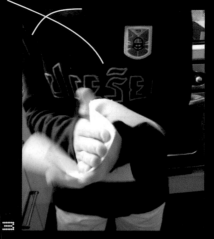

Bend the knees-y, easy-peasy.

Great!

At last I get to eat it.

Easter eggs

Here's a wholesome and easy activity for the little cherubs at Easter time. All you will really have to do is find an egg-shaped mould from a specialist store or supplier to the trade.

Makes 4 easter egg halves,
each about 10 cm (4 inches) long
Preparation time: 25 minutes
Cooling time: 40 minutes

450 g (1 lb) dark, white or milk chocolate
1 packet of breakfast cereal
or 2 packets of crispy buckwheat pancakes
or wafer biscuits, crushed

Melt the chocolate in a microwave oven, a bain-marie or bowl placed over a pan of hot water.

Combine the melted chocolate with the cereal or pancake pieces until they are thoroughly coated with chocolate.

Now you have a choice:

– either fill the moulds completely to make solid egg halves;

– or coat the surface of the moulds with a layer of the mixture to make hollow egg halves.

The first option is definitely the easiest for children; the second requires a little dexterity. Start at the centre of the mould, gradually adding more mixture to 'build up' the sides. Take care not to press the mixture down too hard against the sides of the mould so that the egg does not lose its appealingly rustic, home-made look.

Leave the eggs to cool and set in a refrigerator for about 40 minutes. Twist the mould as you would an ice-cube tray to release the egg halves and turn them out.

Decorate with ribbons. The children can wrap their masterpieces in Cellophane, make pretty labels and give them as presents.

1 Dark, white or milk chocolate - the choice is yours.

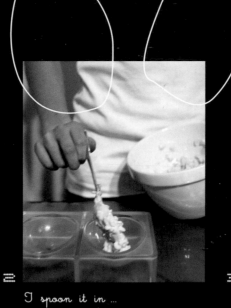

2 I spoon it in ...

3 ... again ...

4 ... and again.

6598-83

5 Press down firmly against the sides of the mould

6 And leave to set. I can't wait!

Jules' veal medallions

1

Everything must be in place.
Tell me if you can't follow anything.

5

You've got to watch it
constantly.

6

I seal them, then turn one
over.

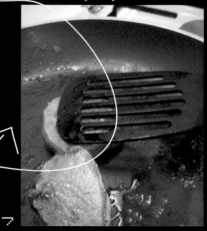

7

And the other one.

9

Put them on a plate.

10

Deglaze the frying pan with the lemon juice, then add a little cream
and pour over the meat.

11

Your hob is a bit too high.

The butter is sizzling.

I turn down the heat.

A sprinkling of sea salt.

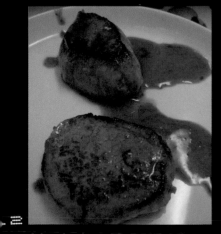

We should take a photo for a cookbook, don't you think?

007

Nicolas's yogurt cake

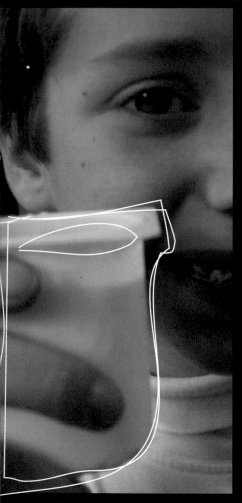

Choose your weapon.

Start with the yogurt.

Then the sugar.

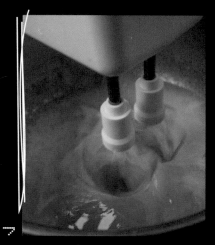

Mix well.

Measure out the flour.

Pour the mixture into the loaf tin without wasting a drop.

Use the same-sized carton for all the weighing out:

1 small carton natural yogurt
2 small yogurt cartons sugar
1 tablespoon brown sugar
1 teaspoon vanilla essence
pinch of salt
3 eggs
3 small yogurt cartons of plain flour
3 teaspoons baking powder
a few drops of lemon juice
125 g (5 oz) unsalted butter, melted

Preheat the oven to 180°C (350°F), gas mark 4.

Empty the yogurt into a bowl.

Add the sugar, brown sugar, vanilla essence and salt.

Beat well with an electric mixer until the ingredients are well mixed.

Incorporate the eggs one at a time, beating well.

Sift in the flour and baking powder. Add the lemon juice.

Finally, add the melted butter.

Stir well, then pour into a buttered, floured loaf tin.

Bake in the preheated oven for 40–50 minutes, let cool, then tuck in!

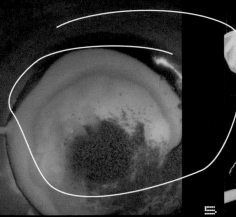

4 A little brown sugar.

5 A quick whiz with the mixer.

6 A few eggs.

9 Add the melted butter.

10 Grease and flour the loaf tin well.

11 40 minutes later ...

Fussy eaters

We all know people whose children tasted their first jugged hare at the age of three, shelled their first lobster at four and wolfed down their first Michelin-starred taster menu at five. Children who won't eat mash unless it's made with a particular variety of potato, the best non-pasteurized crème fraiche, organic butter, Maldon sea salt and crushed Szechuan peppercorns. In another couple of years, they will be taking care of the shopping and cooking their own gastronomic dinners. They'll be the ones making sure they get the correct amount of proteins, fibre, slow sugars, dairy products, iron and vitamin B12.

Sometimes we feel we are the only ones whose children are not discerning gourmets and are fussy eaters. But even if they refuse to eat green beans because they are too long or are not drowned in tomato ketchup, all is definitely not lost.

Here are a few tips, drawn from the experience of people who have been down that particular road.

Tempting tiny tastebuds

It's best to introduce ingredients that are not popular with your children gradually. So therefore use the following in moderation:

1
2
3
4
5

Pick your moment

Leave the 'so you know I love you' for the pets and find other non-food related moments and gestures to express your affections.

Guilt

'I haven't seen them all day, so I'm not going to scold them for that.'
You are on the slippery slope. Stand firm.

Misplaced nostalgia

'But sweetheart, I used to love sautéed veal brains with parsley, garlic and capers when I was little. You know, you're not making me happy. When I tell Grandma…'

Food as a reward or comfort

This may be an excellent technique for training sea lions, but it is totally ineffective with children. Forty years further down the line, they will be throwing themselves on a Mars bar as soon as anything goes the least bit wrong at work.

Your diet

Even if you yourself are eating nothing but mashed avocado and chicken breast, it is important to give your children a 'normal' diet.

Stop being afraid of your child minder or nanny

Tell your child minder once and for all that you do not want your children to have the burger-chips-Coke-chocolate-sundae set meal any more, even if they love it. Brief her well on the 'positive attitude' to be adopted with regard to steamed broccoli and fillet of sole.

Feign indifference

They won't starve. I know, I know, it seems terribly old-fashioned, even cruel, in a world where it is our constant duty to listen, enter into dialogue with, respect and give free choice to our children. But, according to my favourite paediatrician, who has five children aged from 5 and 25, this is the method that produces the most spectacular results with children (including the Deseine children).

Start meals with the vegetables and insist that they eat just a small spoonful of the hated vegetable.

I learned this obvious, yet brilliant tip from my sister-in-law. I started with a single lettuce leaf, and now two of my four children love it. Well, 50% isn't bad!

Your children must be 'eager' at mealtimes

They must be hungry! Avoid giving them enormous teas when they get home from school or late breakfasts. A slice of bread and butter with a few squares of chocolate, a yogurt and an apple, or a chocolate biscuit and a glass of milk is enough. They must also want to share a pleasant, relaxing moment. To help them associate mealtimes with pleasure, take them to a 'grown-ups' restaurant as often as possible. Order a very simple dish with a dessert. Let them have Coke to drink for once, but insist on good manners.

One novelty at a time

Try just one new taste or one new ingredient at a time and always mix them with dishes 'that go down well'.

Keep your cool

Make sure that a 'minimum level of service' is applied in terms of educational and nutritional principles. You'll find everything will sort itself out when they reach the age of 8 to 10 – that's the voice of personal experience speaking, and how I wish that someone had told me that sooner!

Baby peppers stuffed with ketchup rice

Serves 4
Preparation time: 5 minutes
Cooking time: 25 minutes, including rice

4 baby peppers
150 g (5 oz) cooked rice
4 teaspoons tomato ketchup

Preheat the oven to 180°C (350°F), gas mark 4.

Cut across the stalk end of each pepper to make a lid. Scrape out the seeds and membranes.

Combine the rice with the tomato ketchup and spoon into the peppers.

Bake in the oven for 10–15 minutes.

You can also sprinkle a little Parmesan or Gruyère cheese over the rice before cooking in the oven.

Generally, ketchup rice goes down without any difficulty. Take advantage of that fact to try to make them eat the pepper container.

I have seen many children so taken with baby vegetables that they will actually try them, although going on to leave a clean plate is a different matter altogether.

It's a fact: if there's one soup vegetable-hating children will probably like, it's pumpkin soup. Like tomato and carrot, it tempts them with its very sweet taste. Use it as a base and vary the garnishes.

Pumpkin soup

Serves 4
Preparation time: 5 minutes
Cooking time: 20 minutes

750 g (1½ lb) pumpkin, diced
200 ml (7 fl oz) single cream
salt and freshly ground black pepper

Cook the pumpkin in boiling water for about 20 minutes. When very soft, liquidize it in a blender with a little cooking water to produce a very thick purée.

Add the cream, then season to taste. Serve on its own or with grated Parmesan, garlic croutons, chorizo sausage or grilled bacon.

Tomato soup

Serves 4
Preparation time: 5 minutes
Cooking time: 25 minutes

2 tablespoons olive oil
2 onions, chopped
1 garlic clove, crushed
1 teaspoon sugar
1 kg (1¾ lb) very ripe tomatoes, skinned, deseeded and quartered
salt and freshly ground black pepper

Heat the olive oil in a saucepan and fry the onions and garlic with the sugar. Add the tomatoes, season lightly, and leave to simmer for about 25 minutes.

Purée the soup in a blender. Serve hot or cold with all sorts of garnishes that the little cherubs will want to try.

Melon and chorizo soup

Serves 4
Preparation time: 10 minutes

2 Charentais melons, very ripe
about 15 thin slices of chorizo, cut into bite-sized pieces

Scoop out the melon flesh and purée in a food processor.

Place the soup in a refrigerator. When it is very cold, top with the slices of chorizo and serve immediately.

Mangetout peas with peanuts

What's that green stuff under the peanuts?

Serves 4
Cooking time: 3 minutes

150 g (5 oz) mangetout peas
2–3 tablespoons dry-roasted peanuts

Steam or boil the mangetout for only a few minutes so that they are still crunchy. Crush the peanuts and sprinkle over the mangetout before serving.

Baby squash with herb butter

If the herbs in the butter are perhaps a little ambitious, just leave it plain.

Serves 4
Preparation time: 5 minutes
Cooking time: 3–5 minutes

1 tablespoon snipped chives or chervil
30 g (1 oz) butter
about 12 baby squash
freshly ground black pepper

Combine the herbs with the butter, then keep in a cool place. Steam or boil the squash for 3–5 minutes.

Top with a knob of butter and serve with a smile.

Honey-roasted winter vegetables

Serves 4
Preparation time: 5 minutes
Cooking time: 20–25 minutes

400–500 g (13 oz–1 lb) mixed winter vegetables, diced (such as carrot, pumpkin, celeriac, parsnip and potato)
3–4 tablespoons olive oil
2 tablespoons clear honey
sea salt and freshly ground black pepper

Preheat the oven to 180°C (350°F), gas mark 4.

Place the vegetables in an ovenproof dish. Combine the oil with the honey, then pour over the vegetables, turning them to ensure they are thoroughly coated.

Roast for about 20–25 minutes, turning occasionally, until deliciously caramelized. Season to taste.

Cream of salmon and sweetcorn soup

Serves 4
Preparation time: 5 minutes
Cooking time: 5 minutes

knob of butter
1 leek, white part only, sliced
1 tablespoon plain flour
about 500 ml (17 fl oz) water
salt and freshly ground black pepper
300 g (10 oz) organic salmon fillet, diced
1 medium can sweetcorn, drained
150 ml (¼ pint) single cream

Melt the butter in a saucepan
and fry the leek. Add the flour
and cook for 1 minute.

Add the water and bring
to the boil. Season with
salt and pepper.

Add the salmon and
sweetcorn and cook
for a few minutes.

Add the cream, stir
and serve.

Duck with cherries (fruit = vegetables)

Serves 4
Cooking time: 10 minutes

2 tablespoons olive oil
2–3 duck breasts, sliced
500 g (1 lb) sweet cherries
sea salt and freshly ground black pepper

Heat the oil in a frying pan and brown the slices of duck breast. When sealed on both sides, reduce the heat and add the cherries to the frying pan.

Cook gently for a further 5 minutes, stirring so that the duck absorbs the flavour from the cooking juices from the cherries.

Season to taste and serve immediately.

Cooked wheat with sea salt, good quality freshly ground black pepper and Parmesan

A dish discovered by a dad who was having difficulty getting his children to eat anything other than pasta for tea. He still hasn't told them it's wheat, but at least he moved things on without drowning the dish in tomato ketchup or rubber masquerading as grated Gruyère cheese.

Serves 4
Cooking time: 5 minutes

1 bag frozen cooked wheat, or 4 portions wheat cooked according to the instructions on the packet
sea salt and freshly grated black pepper
freshly grated Parmesan cheese

Season the 'pasta' with the salt, pepper and Parmesan.

179

Crab lasagne with butter and citrus fruit

Serves 4
Preparation time: 10 minutes
Cooking time: 15 minutes

250 g (8 oz) crab meat, fresh if possible or vacuum-packed, available from the fish counter
2 oranges, peeled and cut into quarters, and 1 grapefruit, peeled and cut into pieces
8 sheets lasagne
75 g (3 oz) butter, plus a little extra for frying
1 shallot, very finely chopped
juice of 1 orange
freshly ground black pepper

Combine the crab meat with the orange quarters and grapefruit pieces and set aside.

Cook the lasagne strips in salted boiling water until just tender (al dente).

Heat a knob of butter in a saucepan and fry the shallot, not allowing it to colour. When it is soft, add the orange juice and reduce until it is slightly syrupy. Add the remaining butter, a little at a time, beating in each addition with a whisk to lightly thicken the sauce.

Add the fruit and the crab meat to the sauce, season with the pepper, then heat very gently.

Drain the lasagne, place a strip on each plate and place 1 tablespoon of the crab mixture on each strip. Cover with the remaining sheets of lasagne and top with the remaining crab sauce.

Sardine flan

Serves 4
Preparation time: 3 minutes
Cooking time: 20 minutes

4 sheets of ready-made puff pastry
2 tablespoons sun-dried tomato preserve
2 tomatoes, finely sliced
2 cans sardines in oil

Preheat the oven to 180°C (350°F), gas mark 4.

Place the rolled out pastry pieces on a greased baking sheet. Spread the tomato preserve over the pastry, arrange the tomato slices and top with the sardines. Bake in the oven for 15–20 minutes.

Multi-coloured omelette

I often read that children love colour and that we should take advantage of that fact to get them to eat vegetables. Despite being very pretty, in our house it is still mum and dad who always finish off the omelette. Let me know if it works better for you.

Serves 6
Preparation time: 10 minutes
Cooking time: 10–15 minutes

2 tablespoons olive oil
1 yellow pepper, finely sliced
1 orange or red pepper, finely sliced
12 eggs
200 ml (7 fl oz) full-fat milk
50 g (2 oz) freshly grated Parmesan cheese
1 carrot, finely sliced using a paring knife
salt and freshly ground black pepper

Heat the olive oil in a frying pan and fry the peppers for 5 minutes.

Beat the eggs together with the milk, then add the Parmesan. Add the sliced carrot, together with a little salt and pepper, then pour the mixture into the frying pan with the peppers. Cook over a low heat for 10–15 minutes.

Before serving, place the frying pan under a hot grill to brown the top of the omelette.

My children love mussels, while I love the fact that they love them. As this dish takes concentration and time to sort out when they're eating, it ensures that peace reigns in the restaurant, not to mention the admiring look from people sitting nearby. And if, to boot, the mussels have had the good idea of giving a lift to baby crabs, I can count on twice as much time thanks to the highly scientific experiments of four budding Dr Frankensteins!
You should see what they're like with langoustines!

Mussels with coconut

Serves 4
Preparation time: 20 minutes
Cooking time: 10 minutes

2 shallots, finely chopped
knob of butter
1 kg (1 ¾ lb) mussels, cleaned
1 glass dry white wine
400 ml (14 fl oz) can coconut milk

Fry the shallots in the butter, but do not allow to colour. Add the mussels and then the wine and cook over a high heat for about 5 minutes. Discard any mussels that have not opened.

Stir the mussels well, add the coconut milk and stir again. When the liquid is very hot, serve immediately.

Mini-cheese board

Once again take advantage of the marketing people to present a mini-cheese board just like the one for the grown-ups. It will greatly increase your chances of seeing your children trying several different cheeses.

Viking milk

Serves 1 child who doesn't much like milk
Preparation time: 1 minute

1 egg yolk
2 teaspoons sugar
1 glass milk

Beat the egg yolk with the sugar and milk.

Serve to your child, while telling them that this was the powerful drink that made the Vikings so strong and handsome.

Smoothies

An excellent way of cramming in the daily 5 portions of fruit and vegetables.

Invest in a beautiful juicer that will also enhance your kitchen, and fill your freezer with a selection of frozen fruit (such as raspberries, mango, apricot, citrus fruits) if you can't buy them in season or haven't the time to prepare them.

There are not many culinary activities that give my children as much pleasure as just pressing the button to pulverize ingredients of all sorts of colours and then transforming them into a smooth magic mixture. Fine, just so long as there's no frog involved!

Mixed with yogurt or milk, they make delicious iced milk shakes, far better than bought ones or those available in fast-food chains.

Here are a few of my family's winning combinations.

Apricots and vanilla yogurt drink

You can thin this mixture down with milk or orange juice.

Mango, raspberry, pineapple, banana

No need to add any dairy produce as the banana makes it wonderfully smooth.

Apple and cranberry

Peel and dice the apple and whiz with fresh cranberry juice.

Cherry and chocolate

With a little full-fat milk and grated chocolate to taste.

Macaroons

Make them as flat or as rounded as you like. Either way, they will still be beautifully soft. They are gluten free and contain no cow's milk.

Makes about 12
Preparation time: 10 minutes
Cooking time: 15 minutes

2 egg whites
125 g (4 oz) soft brown sugar
125 g (4 oz) ground almonds or hazelnuts

Preheat the oven to 180°C (350°F), gas mark 4.

Whisk the egg whites into very stiff peaks.

Fold in the sugar, followed by the almonds (or hazelnuts) using a metal spoon so that the egg whites do not collapse.

Spoon small mounds of the mixture onto a sheet of greaseproof or silicon paper placed on a baking sheet, then bake for 12–15 minutes.

Remove the macaroons from the oven and leave to cool.

Strawberry soup with fromage frais

Serves 4
Preparation time: 3 minutes

500 g (1 lb) ripe and flavoursome strawberries
2–3 tablespoons sugar
4 small pots fromage frais

Hull the strawberries and purée them in a food processor with the sugar.

Pour into a shallow dish and turn the pots of fromage frais out into the strawberry soup.

Acknowledgements

Shopping and table decoration: Pauline Ricard-André

Paper plates

Cutlery
Ikea – p.31, p.52, p.73
Surplus Doursoux – p.41

Plates, dishes and saucepans
Bodum – p.8, p.10, p.21, p.24, p.27, p.31, p.35, p.37, p.39, p.43, p.57, p.58, p.71, p.76, p.78
Surplus Doursoux – p.41, p.124, p.125, p.126, p.129, p.130
Ikea – p.10, p.12, p.52, p.59, p.70, p.79, p.82, p.85, p.87, p.108, p.138, p.174, p.175, p.179
Luminarc – p.17, p.53, p.184, p.187

Bowls and glassware
Bodum – p.4, p.18, p.143, p.178
Luminarc – p.21, p.23, p.55, p.56, p.78, p.175
Ikea – p.48, p.58, p.73, p.74, p.77, p.107, p.143

Tablecloths, fabrics, table mats and accessories
Antoine & Lili – p.24, p.27, p.33, p.35
Périgot – p.135, p.141

Trays
Ikea – p.25, p.61, p.99, p.101

Address book

Antoine & Lili	Online sales:	www.altribu.com
Bodum	Bodum Home Store, 24 Neal Street, Covent Garden, London WC2 9PS	Tel. 0207 240 9176
Ikea	Online sales and information:	www.ikea.co.uk
La Piñata	25, rue des Vinaigriers, 75010 Paris	Tel. 00 33 (0)1 40 35 01 45
	Piñata party games also available online from:	www.partybox.co.uk
Luminarc	(on sale in department stores and specialist shops)	
Périgot	16, rue des Capucines, 75009 Paris	Tel. 00 33 (0)1 53 40 98 98
Surplus Doursoux	3, passage Alexandre, 75015 Paris	Tel. 00 33 (0)1 43 27 00 97

For cake decorating equipment:
www.jane-asher.co.uk/sugarcraft.asp
www.wilton.com

Kooks Unlimited, 16 Eton Street, Richmond, Surrey TW9 1EE
Tel.: 0208 332 3030

Thanks to:

– Sylvain for having the patience of a saint
– all the Marabout team
– Dr Gilles Valleur
– Fiona for her valuable advice
– Jacqueline, avant-garde nanny and so much more
– Arthur, Zoé, Jules A, Philippine, Colette, Maxence, Octave, Elliott, Emile, Axel, Hugo, Pauline, Clément, Nicolas B, Jules C, Adèle, Nicolas P, Cécilia, Alice, Marie-Charlotte, Perrine, Erin, Margo, ML, Odile, Pierre Louis, Nathalie, Virginie, Thierry, Patrick and Marie for being so willing and happy to get involved.

Txx

Managing editor: Elisabeth Darets
Managing art editor: Emmanuel Le Vallois
Graphics: Nathalie Delhaye
Production: Laurence Ledru
Proof-reading: Antoine Pinchot.

© Marabout (Hachette Livre), 2004
This edition published by Hachette Illustrated UK,
Octopus Publishing Group Ltd.,2–4 Heron Quays, London E14 4JP

English translation by JMS Books LLP
(email: moseleystrachan@blueyonder.co.uk)
Translation © Octopus Publishing Group Ltd.

A CIP catalogue for this book is available from the British Library

ISBN-13: 978-1-84430-121-8

ISBN-10: 1-84430-121-4

Printed in Singapore by Tien Wah Press

Recipe index

Index + acknowledgements